GOLDEN DREAMS

True Stories of Adventure in the
California Gold Rush

FRANK BAUMGARDNER

ARCHWAY
PUBLISHING

Archway Publishing books may be ordered through booksellers or by contacting:

Archway Publishing
1663 Liberty Drive
Bloomington, IN 47403
www.archwaypublishing.com
1 (888) 242-5904

Because of the dynamic nature of the Internet, any web addresses or links contained in this book may have changed since publication and may no longer be valid. The views expressed in this work are solely those of the author and do not necessarily reflect the views of the publisher, and the publisher hereby disclaims any responsibility for them.

Any people depicted in stock imagery provided by Getty Images are models, and such images are being used for illustrative purposes only.
Certain stock imagery © Getty Images.

ISBN: 978-1-4808-8676-6 (sc)
ISBN: 978-1-4808-8677-3 (e)

Library of Congress Control Number: 2020900355

Print information available on the last page.

Archway Publishing rev. date: 03/04/2020

For Jeannette, my beloved, whose love gave me hope.
She never gave up, keeping sacred her vows, and put my
crazed mind at rest—and all in proper perspective.

CONTENTS

FOREWORD

Many accounts of California's Gold Rush focus on one aspect, or one person's account. This book, *Golden Dreams: True Stories of Adventure in the Gold Rush*, weaves together a myriad of experiences of those who made the journey to pre-Statehood California and the gold fields. Overland journeys and sea journeys tell different stories, encounters with Indians and early settlers, illuminate the Gold Rush in different ways. Once the gold seekers arrived in California, they often went in many different directions – this book makes this clear and explains why.

Golden Dreams focuses on the forty-niner's own words – words which were written on the trail or on a ship, and then words written after their arrival. These accounts were written in the mines, by candlelight, hurriedly after a long day's work in the mines – and then sometimes after their trip when they returned home. The successes and failures are both shown, the varied backgrounds of the miners are illustrated and these stories themselves make clear why the Gold Rush had such a strong draw for men and women from all over the world.

Using primary sources and published accounts of diaries, Frank Baumgardner has made this book more immediate for readers. The juxtaposition of the many stories make for not only exciting reading, but also clearly illustrate why gold seekers risked their lives and left their families and friends to seek gold in California.

Patricia L. Keats
Director of Library and Archives
The Society of California Pioneers

PREFACE

Before the gold rush, gold in any great quantity was rare in the existing United States except for a limited strike in North Carolina at the end of the eighteenth century. Before January 1848. Russia was where most of the world's supply of gold was found. When volcanic action created both the Rocky Mountain Chain and the Sierra Nevada Mountain Chain, molten gold spewed out and ran down into numerous California riverbanks, cracks in rock, and gullies, where it mixed with granite and other hard rocks. The gold and silver deposits were laid down millions of years before 1848, and thus placers preexisted the invasion of miners. When gold was found at Coloma (Sutter's Mill) in northern California, news of it spread like a wildfire during the spring and summer of 1848. To most hardheaded people, it didn't seem possible. Wasn't this too good to be true? And yet, as the weeks and months flew by, news article after news article kept stating there was gold and some placer miners were getting rich.

A Honolulu newspaper, *Polynesian,* reported on July 8, 1849,

> **The Gold Fever.** The California *alias* gold fever is beginning to rage with unprecedented fury among the denizens of our town. One after another comes to request us to announce their intention to depart from this Kingdom. The promulgation of the law respecting passports came at an unlucky time for some ... In the emergence of the occasion, creditors will do well to watch their interests closely, for it is impossible to tell who will go next.[1]

Soon the news spread to Central and South America, Hawaii, Australia, China, and the Western European nations as well. Golden dreams seized the minds, hearts, and imaginations of tens of thousands of people worldwide.

---

[1] See "The Gold Fever Article," *Polynesian*, July 8, 1849, no page number," "California Gold Rush—Topics on Newspapers.com," "Articles and Clippings about the California Gold Rush," accessed online on October 10, 2019.

There seemed to be no restrictions to making the journey to California's hilly gold fields. Those who could make themselves free could come. It apparently made no difference what faith one practiced, where someone came from, or what color of skin one happened to bear.

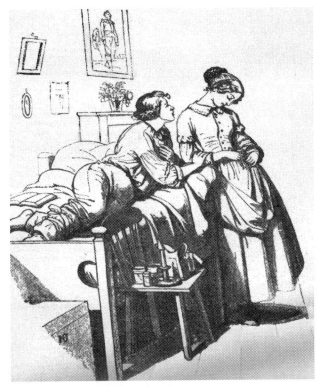

"Will you go the caper?"

The California gold rush was unique. Nothing in the world like it had ever happened before. By 1855, three hundred thousand people from all over the world flocked to remote California. Thousands came from Europe, China, Latin America, and Australia. For the Indians of the soon-to-be new state, it was disastrous. Although they were of great assistance to the miners, thousands died from starvation, disease, or genocide.

Although the news about California's gold deposits reached the minds of all, not everyone could take on the difficult journey to reach the distant, just-acquired territory, which was full of surprises. Forty-niners, out on the

California Trail, found pans of water left the night before, frozen solid in the morning. Cattle might suddenly be gone, having wandered away or been taken by Indians. Some who decided to go by sea, like Nelson Kingsley, a gold-seeker from Connecticut, passed around Cape Horn. Kingsley noted that his ship's main mast was broken in two. Passengers and crew jerry-rigged the mast together in order for the ship to limp into a nearby port in southern Chile. Once an emigrant left home and began the caper, he or she could rarely turn back. It has been estimated that of the three hundred thousand gold seekers, about half came by sea, and half came overland.

The California gold rush, in its most feverish pitch, lasted only about three years. If one arrived in 1852 or later, one was almost too late. The gold placers, flakes and nuggets, or whole chunks of pure gold—the stuff of fantastic visions and nightly dreams—had already been removed from California's ravines, hills, riverbeds, creeks, and valleys. Gold claims were the financial and legal grist for clever bankers and lawyers, and a federal court system didn't exist anywhere in the Far West.

In this study, many gold seekers are presented not by an academic writing in the third person but by the forty-niners themselves. Their diaries tell their stories. In addition, the study primarily focuses on the northern California diggings. For as long as I can remember, I've thought about writing a book like this. The problem for me was getting the time for research and writing. Previously, I was too busy earning a living. Although accounts like these were written, books containing them are missing from libraries. Most publishers of such accounts are long since out of business. I had to buy most of the diaries from a rare book store in San Francisco, The Argonaut Book Store.

Parts of these diaries made up the text. Many of these miners, working almost twenty-four-seven in extreme heat or cold, as well as rainy or snowy weather, fell ill. Placer mining work was so physically taxing that they turned to other occupations. Some had worked as newsmen before they'd journeyed here, and they returned to plying their trade to write travel accounts or how-to books, which were sold to the general public. Many found the circumstances of life so lonely that they perished from heartbreak. Others succumbed to diseases: cholera, smallpox, influenza, dysentery, malaria, or accidents. Only the most fortunate could take stock of their situations to sell out and return to their families, loved ones, and friends. Far fewer ever returned with a sufficient pile and made any really significant gain in social position, which all miners had desired before leaving their homelands. Often, if they did make it back in one piece, they were so weak or sickened that they died soon afterward.

It was the gold rush that brought this beautiful, remote land of California to be eternally known as "the golden state." The forty-niners were risk takers. Some, like Sterling B.F. Clark, succeeded beyond their dreams only to pay with their lives. Others were desperate criminals. Like our own, the forty-niners' stories were remarkable tales of perseverance, courage, dedication, and fortitude. They didn't make excuses, complain, or blame anyone else for dying or failing. If and when mining didn't work out, many turned to other types of employment.

We owe the miners, whose diaries gave us their stories in this book, a great deal of thanks. They, and they alone, are the ones who truly deserve credit for leading the wave of emigrants who settled the West. The example they set as pioneers is our sacred eternal heritage. Their dreams, desires, dedication to their coworkers, perseverance, hard work, and passions are what still differentiate America and its people from any other country today.

MAIN CHARACTERS

1. Lieutenant Colonel James Mason, commander of the First Dragoons (Cavalry) US Army

2. Reverend (Mayor) Colton, first American mayor (alcalde) of Monterey; copublisher along with Robert Semple of *The Californian,* California's first English language newspaper

3. Vicente Perez Rosales, elder member of the Perez Rosales family of Chilean forty-niner immigrants to the California gold mines in 1849.

4. E. (Edward) Edward Buffum, member of the US Army's First New York Regiment; service in Baja California; early gold miner

5. Sterling B. F. Clark, successful forty-niner; immigrated to the northern California gold miners cross-country route in 1849; pioneer

6. Edward Chever, pioneer and cofounder of Yuba City, merchant, argonaut by way of the Straits of Magellan

7. Alonzo Delano, pioneer from upstate New York, distant relative of President FDR, newsman, mine co-owner, humorist, immigrant by cross-country route

8. Edward M. Prime, adventurer from Wisconsin, cross-country route, miner; returned home to write his story; later visited Pike's Peak; later life unknown

9. James Delevan, publicist of California mining, California adventurer; argonaut from New York to Panama, across the Isthmus to Panama, then by ship north to San Francisco; toured both northern and southern mining districts

10. Samuel McNeil, publicist of California mining; Lancaster, Ohio, shoemaker; husband and father; bar owner and manager in Sacramento; riverboat down Mississippi River; by ship to Mexico; crossed northern Mexico; ship from Mazatlan, Mexico to San Francisco

11. Israel and Titus Hale, father and son forty-niners from Missouri, successful, returned to wife and children with mining proceeds; Titus was an early head of the California Pioneer Society

12. Nelson Kingsley, musician; expert Connecticut carpenter; emigrant via the brig *Anna Reynolds;* forty-niner, 1849–1852; moderately successful, returned and married his fiancée

13. Robert Stedman, Massachusetts forty-niner; builder of many ranch homes in Marin County; pioneer

14. Edward Chever Co-founder Yuba City, pioneer, argonaut, Store owner, merchant

15. Alonzo Delano Grass Valley pioneer, city treasurer, newspaperman, Wells Fargo agent, humorist

CHAPTER 1

Colonel James Mason and Reverend Walter J. Colton's First Impressions of the Mines

The most moderate estimate I could obtain from men acquainted with the subject was, that upwards of 4,000 men were working in the gold district, of whom more than one-half were Indians, and that from 30,000 to 50,000 dollars' worth of gold, if not more, were daily obtained.

—Reverend Walter J. Colton, mayor of Monterey, diary entry, late summer 1848

During June 1848, Colonel Mason and Reverend Colton made trips to see what the American River gold-mining district looked like. Before gold was discovered near Coloma, almost everyone who lived on the East Coast, in the Midwest, or in the South thought California was a remote, nearly worthless wilderness at the extreme western edge of North America. To most Americans, it appeared to be a strange region with dangerous grizzly bears and primitive, uncivilized Indians. The majority of California's residents were Mexicans, many of whom owned large rancheros. There was only a sprinkling of foreign-born people, very few of whom were Americans. Some, like John Sutter from Switzerland and Jasper O'Farrell from Ireland, had been born in northern Europe. This desolate territory quickly began to change in late January, 1848 when James Marshall discovered gold at the location of a sawmill he was building. Marshall and his small crew had been employed by John Sutter.

A couple of years before this, the Mexican War had broken out. As a result, California became an American territory during the same month that gold was discovered in northern California. Begun over the southern border of Texas, this war was fought by both American naval and army forces. To be certain, California would be acquired by the United States. Commodore Robert F. Stockton commanded American forces, including Americans under Captain John C. Fremont forced Mexico's General Castro to flee to Sonora, Mexico, instead of making a final stand.

On America's flagship, the *USS Congress,* with Commodore Stockton serving as chaplain, was Reverend Walter J. Colton. Long before this, Reverend Colton had delivered a sermon in the nation's capital, Washington, DC, that had impressed President Andrew Jackson. The president asked Reverend Colton whether he would prefer to become an American consul or be made a navy chaplain. Colton chose the latter. He served in that post when the *USS Congress* arrived in Monterey Harbor. During a lull in the fighting in July 1846, Commodore Stockton appointed Reverend Colton to be the first American mayor (or alcalde) of Monterey.

Up until the time of the American capture of California, which was accomplished in early 1847, Monterey had been Alta California's capital. Its population was composed of mostly Californios.[2] Reverend Colton learned that the people of Monterey loved to dance, play their guitars, drink, and enjoy themselves on weekends. However, there was a difficult case involving an Indian woman who was a Monterey Californio's household servant. The case that came before him to decide as alcalde was over the upbringing of the woman's child. Mayor Colton described what happened in his diary, which was the same diary briefly quoted at the beginning of this chapter. The following excerpt illustrates Mayor Colton's character.

---

[2] *Californio* is a term for people who made up the majority of the resident population of California. In general, their ancestors had come to California by way of Mexico. San Francisco's first Californio residents were in Lt. Colonel de Anza's exploratory party in the 1770s. Many traced their ancestry back to Spain's conquistadors, who had conquered the Aztec Indians. Spain's soldiers, some of whom remained in Mexico, intermarried with Indians. Most nineteenth-century Americans, including Abraham Lincoln, mislabeled them by calling them Spaniards.

An Indian woman of good appearance came to our office to-day stating that she had been for two years past a domestic in a Mexican family near Monterey; that she had during this time, lost her husband, and now wished to marry again; but wished before she did this, to recover her child, which was forcibly detained in the family in which she had served. It appeared that the father of the family had baptized her child, and claimed, according to custom here, a sort of guardianship over it, as well as a right to a portion of its service.

I asked her if her child would be kindly treated where it now was; she said she thought it so; but added, she was a mother, and wanted it with her. We told her as she was going to marry again, she had better perhaps leave the child for the present; and if she found her husband to be a good, industrious man, and disposed to furnish her with a comfortable home, she might call again at our office, and we would get her child. She went away with that mild look of contentment which is as near a smile as any expression which lights an Indian's face.[3]

Twelve days later, on Saturday, August 15, 1848, Alcalde Colton wrote,

To-day the first newspaper [*The Californian*] ever published in California made its appearance. The honor, of writing its Prospectus, fell to me. It is to be issued on every Saturday, and is published by Semple [Robert] and Colton. Little did I think when relinquishing the editorship of the *North American* in Philadelphia, that my next feat in this line would be out here in California. My partner is an immigrant from Kentucky, who stands six feet eight in his stockings. He is in a buckskin dress, a foxskin cap, and is true with his rifle, ready with his pen, and quick at the type-case.[4]

---

[3] *Ibid.,* 5–6.

[4] *Ibid.,* 11. Bear Flag leader Robert Semple was born and raised in Kentucky. In December 1845, he arrived at Sutter's Fort on a mule train. He joined Fremont's Battalion, along with other

American naval and army officers began taking over from Mexicans throughout cities and towns in California. There were convocations to institute new ways of governing. Now there was no going back to the former ways of doing business, where California's residents looked to either Rome or Mexico City for direction. Initially change began slowly yet continuously during the summer of 1846 until late January 1849.

Soon after James Marshall's discovery of gold at Coloma, word about this gold strike spread initially to San Francisco by Sam Brannon and others and then out to the entire world. A series of additional gold strikes took place on Mormon Island and in Weber's Creek in February 1848.

One or two of Marshall's workmen had used their pocketknives to scrape out gold flakes from rocks and crevices. Mining tools of the forty-niners rapidly improved to include handheld pickaxes, pry bars, wheelbarrows, sluice boxes, rockers, Long Toms, even a diving bell. Long Toms were eight- or ten-foot long sluices that required at least three men to operate.

Most of the mining that was done from 1848 through 1855 was surface or placer mining, as opposed to deeper shaft mining. By 1852 and later, the most productive mines were gold mines like the Empire Gold Mine near Coloma, which is now a California state park.

In 1848, prospectors discovered gold at Bidwell's Bar on July 4 and also on the Yuba River. Gold also was found at Mariposa in 1849 and at Rich Bar in Plumas County at the head of the Feather River in 1850. These discoveries brought hordes of new prospective miners, such as the crews of ships that docked at San Francisco. The harbor there was filled with abandoned ships as crewmen left to go to the gold fields. The cliché was, "Time is money." Almost immediately, shipyards on the East Coast began new speedier ships called clipper ships, which held a greater number of sails to improve their speed.

There seemed to be no end to the ongoing stream of riches from California.

At first, however, there were many who doubted the tales about the gold rush. And yet as news of new gold strikes continued to spread, each one richer

---

Bear Flaggers, who marched down to southern California to confront Gen. Castro's Mexican force. He was in Monterey, Alta California's capital, when the US Navy, under Commodore Sloat, brought down the Mexican flag, replacing it with Old Glory. Semple and Mayor Colton continued publishing the first California newspaper, *The Californian*, during 1847.

than the last, gold fever took hold of thousands of new converts every day. People from all walks of life left for California. Women's lovers, sweethearts, those smitten by glassy-eyed males, and even spouses suddenly disappeared. Thousands of women suddenly faced loneliness, disappointment, cold houses, empty beds, despair, and even destitution. The California gold rush was on! The initial phase of it, placer mining, lasted for about five years.

Eventually, some three hundred thousand immigrants rushed to the gold districts, many without any plan or knowledge of where to look for gold. If they happened to be Americans, born in one of the states of the Union, there were four or five possible routes to be taken: by ship around Cape Horn, across Panama or Nicaragua; across the Great Plains, the Rockies, the Sierra Nevada, or even down the Mississippi to New Orleans; by ship to Texas or northern Mexico; by land to Mazatlan; and by ship north to San Francisco. Some even started out to New Mexico and onward by the Gila River route. In addition, many others came from every distant corner of the globe: China, Japan, South and Central America, Mexico, the Sandwich Islands (Hawaii), northern Europe, and Australia. At first, California's residents didn't welcome these brash, mostly American newcomers. Many quickly found ways to adapt, and a few even found ways to profit a little by opening up saloons, casinos, boarding houses, theaters, and hotels.

As for Mayor Walter Colton, the first report of gold's discovery came as a shock. On May 29, 1848, Colton wrote in his diary,

> Our town was startled out of its quiet dreams to-day, by the announcement that gold had been discovered on the American Fork. The men wondered and talked, and the women too, but neither believed.[5]

Monterey lay just 115 crow-flown miles from San Francisco, where residents already were buzzed with news that gold was being recovered only 142 miles due eastward in "them thar hills!"[6]

---

[5] *Ibid.,* 133.

[6] Today, with the aid of freeways and well-designed highways, one can usually drive from the San Francisco Bay Area to Coloma and Placerville in fewer than four hours, if traffic isn't

Still curious, on June 6, 1848, Mayor Colton dispatched a horseman to ride up to the American River to confirm or dismiss the rumor of gold. Two weeks later, Colton's messenger ended all of Monterey's doubts when he emptied gold nuggets out of his pockets in front of the assembled crowd. According to Colton, the messenger

> passed them around among the eager crowd. The family who had kept house for me caught the moving infection. Husband and wife were both packing up; the blacksmith dropped his hammer; the carpenter his plane, the mason his trowel, the farmer his sickle, the baker his loaf, and to tapster his bottle.[7]

Workers employed by Mayor Colton also abruptly quit, leaving for the mines. Some, like one fellow the mayor called "Bob," came back temporarily flush with what seemed like easy money. On August 12, 1848, before he made an excursion to the mines himself, Mayor Colton wrote,

> My man, Bob, who is of Irish extraction, and who had been in the mines about two months, returned to Monterey four weeks since, bringing with him over two thousand dollars, as the proceeds of his labor. Bob, while in my employ, required me to pay him every Saturday night, in gold, which he put into a little leather bag and sewed into the lining of his coat, after taking out just twelve and half cents, his weekly allowance for tobacco.

Mayor Colton then asked Bob,

> How is it, Bob? You brought down with you over two thousand dollars; I hope you have not spent all that; you used to be very saving; twelve and half cents a week for tobacco, and the rest you sewed into the lining of your coat, "Oh yes," replied Bob; and I have got <u>that</u> money yet[.] I worked hard for it; and, the

---

too heavy.

[7] *Ibid.,* 13.

diel [devil] can't get it away; but the two thousand dollars came easily by good luck, and has gone as asily [easily] as it came." Now Bob's story is only one of a thousand like it in California, and has a deeper philosophy in it than meets the eye. Multitudes here are none the richer for the mines. He who can shake chesnuts [chestnuts] from an exhaustless tree, won't stickle about the quantity he roasts.[8]

Before another month ended, Mayor Colton formed a party to visit the mines he'd written about. Even though he knew his job as mayor required him to return soon, he couldn't resist the temptation any longer to have a look for himself at the mining that was going on.

During this summer of 1848, other Americans in government posts, like Army Lieutenant Colonel Richard Barnes Mason, commander of the First Dragoons, who later became the acting governor of California, began writing a report on his tour to the mines to his superior officer, Brigadier General R. Jones, Adjutant-General.

Sir, I have the honour to inform you that, accompanied by Lieut. W.T. [William Tecumseh] Sherman, 3rd Artillery, A.A.A. General, I started on the 12th of June last to make a tour through the northern part of California. We reached San Francisco on the 20th, and found that all, or nearly all, its male inhabitants had gone to the mines. The town, which a few months before was so busy and thriving, was then almost deserted. On the evening of the 24th the horses of escort were crossed to Saucelito in a launch, and on the following day we resumed the journey, by way of Bodega and Sonoma, to Sutter's Fort, where we arrived on the morning of July 2.[9]

[8] *Ibid,* 136.
[9] "Official Report on the Gold Mines," The Virtual Museum of the City of San Francisco, online article, accessed April 6, 2017, 1

After Colonel Mason's party reached Sutter's Fort, he continued his report,

> Along the whole route mills were lying idle, fields of wheat were open to cattle and horses, houses vacant, and farms going to waste. At Sutter's there was more life and business. Launches were discharging their cargoes at the river and carts were hauling goods to the fort, where already were established several stores, a hotel, etc.[10]

Colonel Mason, Lieutenant Sherman, and their party reached the mines on the American River.

> On July 9th we arrived in the neighborhood of the mines, and proceeded twenty-five miles up the American Fork, to a point on it now known as the Lower Mines, or Mormon Diggings. The hill sides were thickly strewn with canvas tents and bush-harbours, a store was erected and several boarding shanties in operation. The day was intensely hot, yet about 200 men were at work in the full glare of the sun, washing for gold-some with pans, some with close woven Indian baskets; but the greater part had a rude machine known as a cradle.[11]

After describing how four men, each performing a different task, worked a six- or eight-foot-long Long Tom to produce gold dust, Colonel Mason continued,

---

[10] Ibid., 2.

[11] Ibid., 2. Cradles, or rockers, were usually made of a wooden frame with a metal screen, or riffles, on the bottom. They were 2.5 to 4.0 feet long. To operate a rocker efficiently took two to three individuals. One stood at one end with a shovel and ore-laden soil at one end, loading. Others rocked the cradle to allow gravity to help separate gold nuggets from soil. Somebody tossed buckets of water to aid the separation process. Heavier gold nuggets were caught in the screen at the bottom. So-called Long Toms were the elongated cradles Colonel Mason may have described in his report, which eventually went to President James K. Polk, who publicized it.

A party of four men, thus employed at the Lower Mines, average 100 dollars a-day. The Indians, and those who have nothing but pans or willow baskets, gradually wash out the earth, and separate the gravel by hand, leaving nothing but the gold mixed with sand, which is separated in the manner before described.

The gold in the Lower Mines is in fine, bright scales, of which I send several specimens.[12]

Colonel Mason met James Marshall, who headed the workmen who made the first discovery of gold on the South Fork of the American River, along with Mr. Spence. Spence explained to Colonel Mason how he had found gold "in the small gullies or ravines that occur in the mountainous region." Other miners including Delavan and Kingsley (in following chapters) also found gold in ravines alongside rivers. Colonel Mason moved to Weber's Creek, another site about "three or four miles below the same mill." Colonel Mason stated,

I struck the stream (now known as Weber's Creek) at the washings of Sunol and Company. They had about thirty Indians employed, whom they pay in merchandise. They were getting gold of a character similar to that found in the main fork, and doubtless in sufficient quantities to satisfy them. I send you a small specimen, presented by this Company, of their gold. From this point we proceeded up the stream about eight miles where we found a great many people and Indians, some engaged in the bed of the stream, and others in the small side valleys that put into it. These latter are exceetingly rich, two ounces being considered an ordinary yield for a day's work. A small gutter, not more than 100 yards by four feet wide, and two or three feet deep, was pointed out to me where two men (W. Daly and Percy M'Coon) before obtained 17,000 dollars' worth of gold.[13]

---

[12] *Ibid.*, 2–3.
[13] Ibid., 5.

The first year of the gold rush was when more gold was produced than at any other time in history. It's worth pausing a moment to reflect upon this fact, which those forty-niners who arrived in the gold regions a bit later realized full well. Returning to Colonel Mason's report to Washington, Captain Weber told the colonel that "he knew that these two men had employed four white men and about 100 Indians" for the hard labor, and after paying them off, the pair had "left with 10,000 dollars' worth of gold." Colonel Mason's journey continued. He saw another ravine where "upwards of 12,000 dollars' worth of gold" was found. He also met two others, Mr. Neligh and Mr. Lyman, who were slightly less successful.

About this point in his report, Colonel Mason may have mixed up his dates a little because Mayor Colton noted meeting Colonel Mason's party on September 29. Or, perhaps it was the mayor's mistake. On September 30, reporting on his own party's travel to the mines, the mayor noted,

> The scenery, as we advanced, became more wild and picturesque. A short distance beyond us lay the richest gold mines that had yet been discovered and nature, as if to guard its treasures, had thrown around them a steep mountain barrier ... [Next, they encountered a plain.] Crossing this, we wound over a rough, rocky elevation, and turned suddenly into a ravine up which we discovered a line of tents glittering in the sun's rays. We were in the gold mines! I jumped from my horse, took a pick, and in five minutes found a piece of gold large enough to make a signet ring. We had the unexpected pleasure of meeting here General Mason and Captain [Sherman] who had arrived the evening before in their tour of observation, and Dr. Ord, recently of the army, and Mr. Taylor, of Monterey. They invited us to their camp and a supper which we enjoyed with a keen relish ... If you want to know what it is to have an appetite, which scruples at nothing and enjoys every thing, travel on horse back and sleep in the open air.[14]

---

[14] Ibid., 250. Mayor Colton published his account in 1850. By then, the army had promoted Colonel Mason to the rank of general, and Lieutenant Sherman was promoted to captain.

Rarely before or after this, in this published version of his original diary, did Mayor Colton convey such personal excitement. Travelers today are still treated to the incredible beauty of California's rugged and hilly landscape. Returning to Colonel Mason's report, he described Sam Brannon's store at Sutter's Fort.

> The principal store at Sutter's fort, that of Brannon and Co., had received in payment for goods 36,000 dollars' worth of this gold from the 1st of May to the 10th of July. Other merchants had also made extensive sales. Large quantities of goods were daily sent forward to the mines, as the Indians, heretofore so poor and degraded, have suddenly become consumers of the luxuries of life ... Flour is already worth, at Sutter's, 36 dollars a-barrel, and will soon be 50. Unless large quantities of breadstuffs reach the country much suffering will occur, but as each man is now able to pay a large price, it is believed the merchants will bring from Chili [Chile] and Oregon a plentiful supply for the coming winter.[15]

The gold rush stimulated businesses like the demand for lumber and for wheat which brought about true prosperity elsewhere. Like Nelson Kingsley and other forty-niners, Colonel Mason misjudged California Indians. In the following observation from Colonel Mason's report dated August 17, 1848, he was more accurate.

> The most moderate estimate I could obtain from men acquainted with the subject was, that upwards of 4,000 men were working in the gold district, of whom more than one-half were Indians, and that from 30,000 to 50,000 dollars' worth of gold, if not more, were daily obtained.[16]

The colonel understood the limits of the army's power in a territory as large as California. His command could not "secure to the Government certain rents or

---

[15] Ibid., 7.

[16] *Ibid.,* 7.

fees for the privilege of securing the gold." Herein, he "resolved not to interfere, but permit all to work freely, unless broils and crimes should call for interference."[17] The gold districts, whether in northern, central, or southern California, set up their own so-called courts, which were far too often unjust according to many current historians and scholars.[18] Vigilante committees and such kangaroo courts dealt quickly, severely, and too often unjustly with crimes. Perhaps as important to the army and to the colonel's duty were facts he noted next.

> Labourers of every trade have left their work benches, and tradesmen their shops; sailors desert their ships as fast as they arrive on the coast; and several vessels have gone to sea with hardly enough hands to spread a sail. Two or three now at anchor at San Francisco with no crew on board. Many desertions, too, have taken place from the garrisons within the influence of these mines, twenty-six soldiers had deserted from the post at Sonoma, twenty-four from that of San Francisco, and twenty-four from Monterey.[19]

Losses in such numbers became an increasingly unsolvable issue facing not only the Army but California society during the period from 1848 until much later, when state and federal courts and police forces took over.

Nonetheless, the initial gold rush period (1848–1852) would be the most promising time to be a placer miner. Tens of thousands of new immigrants were on their way to California as 1848 ended, and they shared an identical dream. Upon returning to his post at Monterey, Mayor Colton's described what he thought was happening.

> The gold mines have upset all social and domestic arrangements in Monterey; the master has become his own servant, and the

---

[17] *Ibid.,* 7.

[18] One has to be careful about applying current standards of justice to the past. Tools of the trade of the modern police, such as fingerprinting, DNA testing, CSI, etc., were not yet invented and thus unavailable to the miners.

[19] *Ibid.,* 7–8.

servant his own lord. The millionaire is obliged to groom his own horse, and roll his wheelbarrow; and the hidalgo-in whose veins flows the blood of all the Cortes-to clean his own boots ... And here am I, who have been a man of some note in my day. Loafing on the hospitality of the good citizens, and grateful for a meal, though in an Indian's wigwam. Why, is this not enough to make one wish the gold mines were in the earth's flaming center, from which they spring? Out on this yellow dust! It is worse than the cinders which buried Pompeii, for there, all high and low shared the same fate![20]

It is almost impossible to miss the irony, and also his anxiety for the future, in the mayor's thoughts. He wasn't alone. Observations of other forty-niners will further illustrate how the effects of the gold rush transformed the quiet, slow. bucolic character of early California in such a profound, rapid, and lasting fashion that many were shocked, perhaps even astounded, and not only by the amount of wealth being extracted.

---

[20] Ibid., 139.

CHAPTER 2

Different Views of the Gold Rush: Vicente Perez Rosales and E. (Edward) Gould Buffum

I asked Pule-u-le if he had ever known of the existence of gold prior to the entrance of white men into the mines. His reply was that when he was born, about forty miles higher up the river, he had, when a boy, picked it up from rocks in large pieces, and amused himself by throwing them into the river.[21]

—Edward Gould Buffum's conversation in a California Indian rancheria with Chief Pul-u-le, late 1848

In less than five years (1848–1852), the gold rush yielded over a billion dollars of gold, from dust and tiny flakes to nuggets and chunks weighing more than twenty pounds. California's population spurted from about 157,000 in early 1848, when the gold rush began, to nearly 500,000, with the influx of 300,000 immigrants from all over the world. By the fourth year, 1852, the forty-niners took out eighty million dollars in pure gold (that is $1.8 billion in 2018 valuation).

The excitement, chaos, and drama of California's gold rush have oft been portrayed. Many if not most historians, focus only on those miners who were born and raised in one of the preexisting states of the Union before the end of the Mexican War (1846–1848). Little attention is usually paid to describing how the forty-niners interacted with others such as the Californios, Kanakans,[22] Chilenos, Mexicans, or Chinese. In most camps, the miners followed a simple set

---

[21] *Ibid.* 34.

[22] People from Hawaii (the Sandwich Islands) were called Kanakan by the Californios.

of rules and regulations, where miners used their pickaxes, shovels, or other mining tools like Long Toms, hoses, cradles, or rockers to ward off intruders tempted to jump their claims. It was an unwritten rule that if a tool was left on a well-worked site, no one but the rightful owner could take over that claim. In the mining regions and during the first months, women were few and far between. Until about 1860, only about 19 percent of those living in California gold-mining towns were females. Most women recorded in miners' diaries were married.

During the short span of only five years (1848–1853), gold mining changed from its initial phase of prospecting and placer, or surface mining (or extraction) by individual miners or mining by small companies of two to twenty miners to a much larger, more complicated industry where the employees (in most cases, single men) received wages of less than fifty cents a day working to locate, extract, process, and refine ore deposits to produce gold ingots.

Those who were often killed in accidents by making perilous journeys to the gold fields after leaving their homes often made great personal sacrifices and endured what oftentimes seemed to be unending hardship, including the possibility of violent sudden death through Indian attack; death from diseases like cholera, scurvy, and yellow fever; suicide; or heartbreak. If they passed from such diseases. it was neither quick nor painless.

A very few happened by good luck to be over the right gold deposit ("pay dirt") at the right time. For the most part, these were the men who started right after the first discovery at Sutter's Mill on January 24, 1848. A fortunate few didn't have to travel the long distances that others did. For example, in May 1848, San Francisco's surveyor, Jasper O'Farrell, together with his brother-in-law Patrick McChristian Jr. and three friends, Jacob P. Leese, Samuel Norris, and William Leahy, staked out a claim on the Yuba River.[23] At the end of August, the five partners left the gold fields with seventy-five thousand dollars' worth of gold (over one million dollars today). Their success might seem great, but for the time it was not unheard of. Each of the five men went back to their previous occupations and did not return to mining.

---

[23] See Frank Baumgardner, *Blood Will Tell: Divvying up Early California from Colonel Juan Bautista de Anza to Jasper O'Farrell* (North Charleston, SC: CreateSpace Independent Publishing Platform, 2014), 151.

Back in 1846, when the Mexican War was declared by Congress late in the year, Edward Gould Buffum volunteered and joined an army unit called the New York Volunteers. His unit arrived in Lower California (Baja California) in March 1847. After serving almost a year of garrison duty, he mustered out. He was fortunate enough to be in San Francisco just after gold was discovered at Sutter's Mill. He and Higgins, also a former soldier, went to northern California's gold district.

In the fall of 1848, one day the two men were hunting game with their rifles for supper when they happened across two Indian women "gathering acorns."[24] The women were doing what they usually did to help support their tribe. Acorn mash was the main staple grain the Pomo, and most other California Indians depended on. "Naked above the waist and covered from their waists to their knees with coyote skins, each one carried a conical-shaped wicker basket ... into which they were placing the acorns, which were scattered ankle deep around them." Higgins spoke to them in vain both in English and Spanish, but "they seized their acorn baskets and ran."[25] The two American men were intrigued. They entirely forgot about hunting and followed the women, the pair of "mountain beauties," back to their Indian rancheria.

> It was located on both sides of a deep ravine, across which was thrown a large log as a bridge, and consisted of about twenty circular wigwams, built of brush, plastered with mud, and capable of containing three or four persons ... We were suddenly surrounded by thirty or forty male Indians, who had their bows and quivers slung over their shoulders, and who stared most suspiciously at us and our rifles.[26]

---

[24] See E. Gould Buffum, *Six Months in the Gold Mines from a Journal of Three Years Residence in Upper and Lower California, 1847-9*, ed. John W. Cauhey (The Ward Ritchie Press, 1958), 30–33.

[25] *Ibid.,* 33

[26] *Ibid,* 33. Despite the output of numerous authors, we have had few published articles or books on the initial contacts made between whites and California Indians, such as this one between Pule-u-le and Higgins and Buffum.

Fortunately for the Americans, one of the Indians spoke Spanish. Quickly Buffum assured him he and Higgins had no hostile intent and offered the Indians a present of "two pounds of musty bread and some tobacco which I happened to have in my game bag."[27] The Indian's name was Pul-u-le.

> I apologized to him for the unfortunate fright which we had caused a part of his household, and assured him that no harm was intended, as I entertained the greatest respect for the ladies of his Tribe, whom I considered far superior in point of ornament, taste, and natural beauty to those of any other race of Indians in the country.[28]

The two American men were outnumbered and were obviously apprehensive about what might happen next. It's possible they were honestly impressed by the Indian women, yet it is also possible that the former soldier wanted to create a positive impression on the Indian chief, Pul-u-le. Having now been reassured that the armed strangers posed no threat to his people, Pul-u-le proceeded to give them a guided tour of the interiors of some of their houses. "During our presence our two female attractions had retired into one of the wigwams, into which Pul-u-le piloted us, where I found some four or five squaws similarly besmirched and clothed, and appeared exceedingly frightened at our entrance."[29]

Now it was Buffum's turn to be surprised. After Pul-e-le told the Indian women how Buffum had praised them, "one of the runaways left the wigwam and soon brought me in a large piece of bread, made of acorns, which to my taste was of a much more excellent flavor than musty hard bread."[30]

---

[27] *Ibid*, 31.

[28] [28] *Ibid.,* 31. Buffum described the Indian women: "Their heads were shaved, and the tops of them covered with black tarry paint, and a huge pair of military whiskers were daubed on their cheeks with the same article." Possibly the women did this to themselves to make themselves look somewhat like men.

[29] Ibid., 32.

[30] Ibid., 33. This act of kindness on the part of this Indian woman stands out as a rare and remarkable recorded incident of white and Indian person-to-person interaction, which may well have been repeated elsewhere before Indian reservations were imposed by Congress on California's Indians beginning about ten years later.

Soon after this, Buffum described how he thought the Indians thought about gold. In 1848, some believed it had no value.

> I asked Pule-u-le if he had ever known of the existence of gold prior to the entrance of white men into the mines. His reply was that when he was born, about forty miles higher up the river, he had, when a boy, picked it up from rocks in large pieces, and amused himself by throwing them into the river.[31]

Although this may have sounded odd to a white gold seeker like Buffum, it reflected Indian beliefs about human beings' place as simply one more creature with a temporal role in the natural world.[32] Buffum and Higgins continued on to the gold fields, where they worked as partially successful miners.

Upon returning home, Buffum published his account in 1850. His travelogue was meant to be a how-to guide for later good seekers who were thinking of emigrating from their homes to the gold mining regions of California.

Another forty-niner who tried his hand in the California gold mines was Vicente Perez Rosales. Although they also arrived in California during the early gold rush, Chileans (or Chilenos) did not fare as well as some Americans did. This wasn't all due to bad luck because they had to fight off claim jumpers, which cost them in time and legal fees. Nevertheless, during the first three years of the gold rush (1848–1851), anyone from nearly any part of the world might at least get by as a gold miner if one worked hard enough and happened upon a deposit of gold.

The enchanting gold news from California had reached most of South America by the end of 1848. Throughout that year, news about rich gold discoveries led thousands of youth, mostly boys and men, to dream of getting rich quick. Vicente Perez Rosales, a forty-two-year-old Chilean who hadn't had much success in his other careers while working in Chile, boarded a passenger

---

[31] Ibid., 34.

[32] For the contrasting Indian vs. "Amer-European" view, see Clara Sue Kidwell, Homer Noley, George E. Tinker, *A Native American Theology* (Maryknoll, NY: Orbis Books, 2003), 38–40.

ship, the bark *Stauelli,* in Valparaiso on December 28, 1848.[33] Together with him were his brothers Ruperto, Cesar, Federico, and Felipe Ramirez Rosales. When it sailed, the ship carried ninety men, fifty-eight females, eight pigs, twelve sheep, three dogs, and seven sailors, as well as many different ideas about the new, strange city they were bound for, San Francisco. As in any ocean voyage, to a certain extent the passengers had bonded together, at least for their trip,

> The preconceptions we had formed of this city [San Francisco] were certainly not favourable. We knew that it had belonged to Spain and Mexico and had gained worldwide attention only the year before ... We were totally surprised when we doubled the point of the anchorage, in rapidly gathering darkness and saw spread before our eyes there like an amphitheater a rather pretty although irregular village strewn with good-looking if rather small homes, some of them worth at least 100,000 pesos.[34]

While it was during the first two months of 1849, a navy squadron was in port to keep order and ready for any foreign power's intrusion. Senor Rosales continued.

> The port was crammed with ships of all kinds and nationalities. A North American warship of three decks, with three corvettes and a transport to make up the squadron, stood guard over the harbor. We felt our way into the anchorage with anchors poised, and very cautiously, as one must do, if not sure of his ground. As we crept forward we passed close to a number of ships and were bombarded with questions in various languages. They all boiled down to this: "Where are you from?" And "How long have you been at sea?" Finally we heard the longed for order, "Heave to!"—and the clank of the anchor chains going down.[35]

---

[33] Edwin A. Beilharharz and Carlos U. Lopez, *We Were 49ers: Chilean Accounts of the California Gold Rush* (Pasadena, CA: The Ward Ritchie Press, 1976), 1–20.

[34] Ibid., 16. In 1849, the Chilean peso was the equivalent of the American dollar.

[35] Ibid., 16. The Stauelli dropped anchor in San Francisco Harbor on February 28, 1849.

Most of the passengers anxiously wondered whether any of the rumors of rich gold finds were true. With that thought in the back of his mind, Rosales came ashore the following day. Immediately he noticed what looked to him to be expensive houses being built for former sailors who had become overnight millionaires. He was amazed at how "unbelievably expensive" liquor was when "compared with Chile."[36] Senor Rosales continued.

> Goods have whatever value the seller wants to set; because the buyer, aware that in California time is money, will buy at sight whatever he needs, without bothering to shop around.[37]

Although Rosales and his brothers were fortunate to be in California this early, it took them more than a week to get up to Sacramento on a tiny boat owned by Sam Brannan. In the case of Senor Rosales, his description of Sacramento was even more poignant than ones made by Americans. He included the fact that there were numerous thickets of vines, snakes, turtles, and abundant salmon. The fish were also noted by other forty-niners, including Buffum and Nelson Kingsley. The Chilean wrote,

> The area chosen for town is a beautiful plain, covered with numerous handsome oaks, lying south of the confluence of the American and Sacramento Rivers. Many hollows full of dry reeds, and small hot ponds where the turtles must be boiling, would suggest that this is an unhealthy place in summertime. There are only four houses made of makeshift lumber and with sailcloth roofs. A few others are going up, and in numberless tents of all sizes and shapes are scattered aimlessly about. Our first objective on landing was to look over the camp and pick the driest spot, near the cliff that bounds the city on the north, and there we set up our elegant tents.[38]

---

[36] Ibid., 17.

[37] Ibid., 17.

[38] Ibid., 21.

Rosales's party members were able to mine some gold, but it wasn't in a large enough quantity. About six months before March 1849, miners on the Yuba River picked up large nuggets of gold. During the fall of 1849 a nine-person party including seven African Americans, led by Major William Downie, discovered a rich gold deposit at the junction of the Downie River and the North Fork of the Yuba River. A boomtown, Downieville, soon sprung up into existence with saloons, fifteen hotels, and eateries. The population grew to five thousand by 1850. At first simply named The Forks, the name Downieville soon replaced it permanently. Law and order, or what passed for it, came about through not-always-just frontier justice. For example, after being found guilty of murder by a hurriedly formed lynch mob jury, a pregnant young Latina lady, Josefa Segovia, was executed by hanging on the Jersey Bridge on July 5, 1849. When Josefa rejected the advances of a white man whose body had been found by miners, this miscarriage of justice began. It is questionable to this day whether she really was guilty. One thing is clear: Josefa Segovia was the only pregnant woman who was ever executed by hanging in California.

As we shall learn from other eyewitness accounts in the following chapters, individual men and women came to mine gold in California's riverbeds, ravines, and hills, but few went home with much, if anything, except their lives and their poignant personal memories. One thing is sure: their work left deep wounds on the land and thus much more environmental damage that may never be cleaned up. Gold rush placer mining later gave way to even greater damaging hydraulic cannons that reshaped vast areas. It also led to the digging of quicksilver mines, which produced mercury and other toxins that poisoned rivers, streams, creeks, and lakes.[39] Mercury was important to the gold refining process to separate the gold from granite, but its aftereffects on immigrant miners from China, Sweden, Wales, Norway, Mexico, and Ireland included loss of teeth and eyes that were swollen for a week or more at a time. Their legacy is contamination in lakes like Clear Lake, Lake County, or, in the case of the Jackson Mercury Mine, four miles north of Guerneville, "mining waste piles

---

[39] For what followed, see Clark Mason, "Quicksilver Mines Boomed in the 1870s," *Santa Rosa Press Democra*, February 5, 2017, A12.

making their way into nearby Wilson Creek, which flows into the Russian River."[40]

After having to go to court and pay lawyers' fees in order to defend his family's mining claims, Vincente P. Rosales eventually returned to Chile. He reported that he did not have any more money with him on his return than he had when he'd departed Chile at the end of 1848, but at least he lived to tell his story.

---

[40] *Ibid.*, A12.

Dividing the Pile

Clark and his wife

Above: Rachel and Sterling B.F. Clark

CHAPTER 3

Sterling B. F. Clark: "How Many Miles from St. Jo?"

Started in the rain and went in the forenoon to Lake Valley, 11 miles, through snow, hail and wind. Stopped in the pleasant sun to dry and get dinner. ... Afternoon. Over the highest ridge, over snow-drifts 20 feet deep, freezing cold, Steep perpendicular rocks. On the rocks in the were left broken 26 wagons. At night cold, freezing. Distance 10 miles. Whole distance 21.

—Sterling B. F. Clark, August 17, 1849, Lake Valley, California[41]

Sterling B. F. Clark was born in Rutland, Vermont, in 1825. He had seven older siblings, but not much else is known about his immediate family. In the introduction to his log, published privately in 1929 by his daughter Ella Clark Mighels, along with an autobiography of James Phelan. An ancestor of Clark's, Hugh Clark, immigrated to Connecticut in 1640. On both sides of his family, ancestors fought against Great Britain in the Revolution.

Many of Sterling B. F. Clark's family members spent much of their working lives in a stone quarry in Rutland, Vermont.[42] Too often, working in a stone quarry was deadly. Workers had to breathe marble dust, which often led to early illnesses like lung cancer. Part of Sterling Clark's motivation in becoming a forty-niner was the "fight or flight" impulse to escape an early death from working in the marble quarry.

---

[41] *Ibid.*, 24.

[42] *How Many Miles from St. Jo? The Log Of Sterling B. F. Clark, with Comments by Ella Sterling Mighelsd, Together with a Brief Autobiography of James Phelan, 1819-1892, Pioneer Merchant* (San Francisco: privately printed, 1929).

As he matured into manhood, Clark studied surveying, printing, and the law. He began his career working as the editor of Huntington, Pennsylvania's small-town newspaper. He lived nearby in the town of Hollidaysburg.[43] There, he met and fell in love with a young lady named Rachel Mitchell. As the news of the California gold strikes was confirmed and reached the East Coast, in March 1849, Clark made up his mind to undertake the long and difficult journey west to St. Joseph, Missouri, twelve hundred miles from Hollidaysburg. He would travel from there across the Great Plains and the Rockies to the California gold fields. He and Rachel decided that while he headed west for California, it would be best if she remained living with her father in Hollidaysburg.

On a separate page of Clark's log, he noted the names, latitudes and longitudes, and altitudes of spots he thought were significant: "Fort Laramie, Summit South Pass Rocky Mountains," Fort Bridger, "Mountain before descending to Salt Lake City from which you have a view of the valley of Salt Lake," and "Mormon City."[44] According to Clark's log, Clark and Captain Joseph Taylor[45] left Hollidaysburg on a stagecoach at 10:00 p.m. on Monday, March 11, 1849. Clark was twenty-four or twenty-five years old.

On Wednesday, March 14, they reached Pittsburgh. They boarded the steamboat *Consignee* on Thursday, traveling down the Ohio River. Before reaching Saint Louis, they caught sight of the sunken steamboat *Caroline*. On March 31, he reached St. Jo. He lost ninety-five dollars by leaving his first company to join another, the Evans' Wheeling company.[46] There, he got so sick that he was confined to a small room. After starting again on April 26, they broke down. Upon reaching Council Bluffs on April 27 or 28, they broke down and "got stuck and helped out 12 or 15 times."[47]

Clark's wagon repeatedly got stuck in mud. Each time, he had to unload and then reload. For some unknown, unrecorded reason, Clark's party returned to St. Jo on Friday, May 4. Their party consisted of four individuals: Clark, Evans,

---

[43] Hollidaysburg is in Blair County in central Pennsylvania. It was settled in 1768. According to the 2010 US census, 5,710 persons live in Hollidaysburg.

[44] *Ibid.,* 27–28.

[45] *Ibid.,* 7.

[46] *Ibid.,* 7.

[47] *Ibid.,* 7.

Dubois, and Irvine. They headed westward and reached Agency on Wednesday, May 9. They went six miles the next day. They were never far from being in trouble, as the following note explains.

> Encamped Friday, 11. Started in morning Sunday, after being helped by a friend and four yoke of oxen. Made 7 miles and got stuck again. Had to unload all our wagon. 32 & 7 = 59, Prairie gently rolling. No wood. Very bad water.[48]

His party's issues continued with getting stuck again. He speculated on possibly having to leave half of his wagon's load behind. His entry for May 13 was poignant because it showed not everything that was happening was bad.

> Sunday, May 13th, made 19 miles. Not much trouble. 53 & 19 = 72. (*Ob.*) Truly we are now where the flowers spring up unsown and waste their sweetness on the desert air Rattlesnakes very plentiful.[49]

At this time, Clark's wagon was following a government train. They crossed Nemahaw on May 16. In the next two days, they crossed the Big Blue and the Little B Rivers. "Saturday, 19th. Made 20 miles. Crossed Little Sandy. About 40 have died on this and on the Independence road with a species of cholera. 170 & 20 = 190."[50]

They joined a train with four other wagons. When he raised his eyes, there was an unending line of wagons ahead of them that stretched to the horizon. He endured a number of cold, miserable nights. His tent provided him little or no protection, so he often tried to sleep in soaking wet clothes and a wet blanket. On Wednesday, June 6, they crossed

> from the South Fork to the North Fork of the Platte River, distance 18 miles. Sublime, picturesque scenery when you come within sight of the North Fork, of high bluffs.

---

[48] *Ibid.,* 8.

[49] *Ibid.,* 9.

[50] *Ibid.,* 10.

Encamped in ash hollow, a deep basin near the river. Seven Indian lodges on river with traders. 469 & 18 = 496.[51]

They passed by Chimney Rock and Scott's Bluff. Their journey continued uneventfully through the Black Hills. On Sunday, July 1, they passed Independence Rock and crossed Sweetwater River. On Tuesday, July 10, they

Came 21 miles and reached Fort Bridger. Encamped at bottom.

Wednesday, 11. Staid [stayed] at Fort Bridger. Got mules shod. (Snake Indians.)

Thursday, 12. Made 14 miles. 1047. Traveling in company with a Missouri train of ox-wagons.[52]

On Monday, July 16, Clark's party pulled into Salt Lake City. Clark did not write anything about what he did while staying there, except to note on July 19, he "stopped and boarded at Taft's. Bathed twice in warm springs."[53] After spending three days there, they left Salt Lake City on July 20.

As longer wagon trains formed up to cross what was known first as "the Great American Desert," Americans became familiar with spots along the Oregon and California Trails. Despite the heat, Clark's health continued to be good. His train passed the Weber River, then Box Elder, and he ferried across Bear River, stopping at Malad Creek on Sunday, July 22.[54] They were making good time relative to many other trains. On the following Sunday, July 29, they "came upon the headwaters of the Humboldt River."[55] They took a slight detour before returning to the Humboldt. After traveling at night, they went "over the hills to Marys River" on August 2.[56] Clark simply recorded the daily

---

[51] *Ibid.*, 14.

[52] *Ibid.*, 19.

[53] *Ibid.*, 20.

[54] *Ibid.*, 20.

[55] *Ibid.*, 21.

[56] *Ibid.*, 21.

mileages traveled on each of the following six days. The total was 158 miles. On Wednesday, August 8, he noted,

> Made 28 miles on Humboldt. Camped on Willows, Echo and Bluffs. Lost canteen. 1792.

> The road on Humboldt very sandy and heavy, increasing as you go down the river; the air constantly filled with the dust.[57]

Following the often bone-dry Humboldt was the most trying part of the cross-country route. It was where many wagons broke down, and their animals often died or had to be left to die. Clark had to leave the Humboldt to find grass for their team on August 9 and 10. On Saturday, August 11, Clark noted that they drove themselves onward both day and night.

> Started in morning to cross the desert. Went 2.5 miles, 5 beyond the sink of the river, where we stopped and got some supper. Started 6 o'clock. Went 17 miles by 11 o'clock, then fed the little hay which I had packed on my pack-mule and slept an hour. Started at one o'clock. 1858.[58]

There can be little or no doubt that by pushing themselves to the very limit of human endurance, Clark and his teammates gained vital time in getting to the gold region before others could. In doing so, on Sunday, August 13, they were still plodding "at sunrise. One mule gave out and we had to leave him."[59] The only water they could find was so full of sulfur that it made them vomit.

* * *

They reached Salmon Trout River on Monday, August 13. On Wednesday, August 15, Clark noted,

---

[57] *Ibid.,* 21.

[58] *Ibid.,* 2

[59] *Ibid.,* 22–23.

Struck and made 18 miles in Salmon Trout River Valley. Rich soil and timber upon the west side up the mountains.

We have been gradually ascending and getting among the Sierra Nevada Mountains.[60]

On Friday, August 17, Clark noted,

Started in the rain and went in the forenoon to Lake Valley, 11 miles, through snow, hail and wind. Stopped in the pleasant sun to dry and get dinner.

Afternoon. Over the highest ridge, over snow-drifts 20 feet deep, freezing cold, Steep perpendicular rocks. On the rocks in the were left broken 26 wagons. At night cold, freezing. Distance 10 miles. Whole distance 21. 1989.[61]

Although they were completely exhausted, they kept moving westward. On Monday, August 20, Clark "went to the Gold Diggings." His party had succeeded in getting there before many other potential miners could. It was going to prove to be well worth all the effort he'd put into his journey. On Wednesday, August 22, Clark "went 20 miles within 5 miles of the city. Sent my baggage to Colloma [Coloma] by Bean & Barnes."[62]

Thursday, August 23, was when Clark first entered Sacramento. His estimates of its population and unofficial founding date were, "The city is just below the confluence of the Sacramento and American Rivers, mostly built of cloth houses, about 700 in number. Population 3500, 3 months ago."[63] On Friday, August 24, he wrote, "Went to town. Saw [New York] Herald 30 June. Heard of the attack upon Rome by the French, Polk's death, &c."[64]

Clark's description matches a number of others, including Nelson Kingsley's,

---

[60] *Ibid.,* 23.

[61] *Ibid.,* 24.

[62] *Ibid.,* 25.

[63] *Ibid.,* 25–26. Sacramento was officially founded on February 27, 1850.

[64] *Ibid.,* 26.

who passed through Sacramento either at this time or a few months later. Clark's log neared his final entry. After two days where he only wrote "in camp," on Monday, August 27, Clark wrote, "Went to Sacramento. Sold my mule for $50. Bought mining tools, &c."[65] He was about to go to one of the richest gold diggings ever found in California or anywhere else. On August 28, he "camped 7 miles from Mormon Island."[66] On the next day, he wrote, "Went to Island and prospected." On Thursday, August 30, he "Went 12 miles up the American Fork to the Sandwich Island diggings & prospected."[67]

On August 31 and September 1, Clark made his last entries to his log. "Came back to Mormon Island." Then, "Commenced gold washing."[68]

Becoming a successful forty-niner and working at placer mining took a combination of good luck, determination, timing, and being at the right place and at the right time with the right tools. Sterling Clark possessed all of these requirements. Already he had traveled farther in his journey to the gold fields than anyone in this study, except for Alonzo Delano.

Unfortunately, Clark's daily record-keeping ended at September 1, 1849. What little we know of Clark's actual mining experiences only can be deduced from his later rise to an influential position during 1850–1851 in northern California.

He found the kind of fortune in gold most of the forty-niners only dreamed of. He used some of the money he netted from his gold mining to buy what his daughter, Ella Sterling Mighels, described in 1929 as "land in Sacramento and San Jose." [69] The properties in Sacramento were both of the present lots where the governor's mansion rests, as well as the one where the state capital is. Clark was appointed alcalde (mayor) of Natoma (Mormon Island). What his daughter also recovered, together with his records of his journey above, were two letters her father had written in California to her mother, Rachel Mitchell, in Hollidaysburg, Pennsylvania, in 1850 and 1851. There are a few extracts that she published after his log in 1929.[70]

---

[65] *Ibid.,* 26.

[66] *Ibid.,* 26.

[67] *Ibid.,* 26.

[68] *Ibid.,* 26.

[69] *Ibid.,* 32.

[70] *Ibid.,* 32.

The following extracts are from two letters Clark wrote Rachel. He wrote the first either in late July or early August 1850. Clark had received a letter from Rachel in which she had affirmed her love for him.

> Here to-night I am writing from California to her who has just assured me by letter, that her love is as constant as mine, and if it be as constant as I believe it to be pure, in a few months I shall meet her once again, never more to part ... It seems as though my affection for you increases every day, for there is hardly an hour, while awake, but that I find myself attempting to depict and picture to my mind a scene which I imagine will be the happiest of my life: the time when I shall return to strike glad hands with you ... I am pleased to hear of your studies and improvement in music with the guitar and the piano.[71]

This letter preceded a shorter one in which Clark made clear his intention to return to Pennsylvania and marry his bride. Mrs. Mighels included the following introductory information.

> The following letter, written in mucilage on blue letter-paper and sprinkled with gold- dust and small nuggets of gold, was sent by Clark to Rachel Mitchell on her birthday. In June, 1929, a descendent of theirs preserved this letter between glass for the future. It in a remarkable state of preservation, the gold-dust virtually intact.

> Natoma, Sep. 1, '50 Midnight

> Dear Rachel,

> The next mail leaves this city on the 14th and I have only time to write a few lines. My health is good as usual. Time passes rapidly her soon a few months

---

[71] *Ibid.*, 32–33.

will have passed away, and very soon shall I be by your side, to enjoy that happy scene which bright anticipation now pictures to my mind.

Write as soon as you receive this.

As always,

Sterling

P.S. Excuse brevity.[72]

Clark's mining success allowed him to go to San Francisco, where he purchased beautiful, expensive jewelry as well as "beautiful crepe shawls" for Rachel.[73] By this time, Clark could well afford to travel to Panama on a deluxe steamer.

Rachel and Sterling defied all the odds by staying true to each other throughout a lengthy romance of more than two thousand miles. Sterling Clark returned to Pennsylvania to marry Rachel. Although Clark wanted Rachel to come on her own to California, her father wasn't willing to permit her to do so. It was the Victorian Era, and most young ladies typically followed their parents' wishes.

After being married, the happy newlyweds spent some time in Pennsylvania saying goodbye to family and friends. They planned to travel to California. Perhaps during his crossing of Panama to reach the Atlantic, Clark may have been infected by a tropical disease. He seemed healthy in the photo taken of him and Rachel after their marriage. It was on their return voyage across Nicaragua to California that Clark was struck by a serious ailment, possibly yellow fever. When their ship docked in San Francisco, he was so sick that he was too weak to walk and had to be carried ashore on a stretcher. By then, Rachel was approximately two months pregnant with their daughter, Ella. The following paragraph is how Ella described her birth and what happened next.

---

[72] *Ibid.,* 37–38.
[73] Ibid., 38.

Seven months after Sterling B. F. Clark's death, his daughter was born, and every man and woman in the town [the mining town of Natoma or Mormon Island] welcomed the father-less babe. All came with gifts, and not to be outdone, some miners from the American River brought a gold-rocker, converted to a cradle and took turns in rocking her to sleep. That was in 1853.[74]

Some individuals' lives end so suddenly and tragically that their closest relations' lives are very adversely affected. Rachel wore black when she arrived on Mormon Island. The court awarded Clark's land to Rachel, his widow, and the two Sacramento lots where the governor's mansion and the state capital went to baby Ella.

Such may have been the case for Mrs. Sterling Clark. However, it would appear that young Ella fared well in spite of the sadly premature passing of her father.

Sterling B. F. Clark's story stands out on its own. Clark accomplished almost everything any other forty-niner dreamed of. In many ways, his story serves as an example to us today in terms of pursuing one's goals despite all the hardships and misfortunes that would have defeated someone of lesser character and determination.

---

[74] Ibid., 40.

Above: Ella Clark Mighels

Above: Edward Prime

CHAPTER 4

Edward M. Prime and
His Wild Goose Chase

They also found one dead Indian near the body [bodies] of four more white men on the sides of the mountain near the road[.] (Vengeance was sworn on every Indian that should make his appearance within rifle shot.) The day twenty six miles and camped on a small creek with good feed and water rushing[,] sage brush for fuel.[75]

—Edward Prime's Journal while lost in Nevada, summer 1850

On the first page of his journal, Edward M. Prime, a native of Linn, in the Lake Geneva region in southeastern Wisconsin, stated that he meant for his diary to be read only by his family members. On March 18, 1850, about six months after Edward Chever had started his Yuba City store, Mr. Prime wrote his first entry. It is possible that later, Prime may have purchased tools or provisions at Chever's store. In the preface to his journal, Mr. Prime wrote,

During the California excitement in the Spring of eighteen hundred fifty, I was suddenly taken with the gold fever (which carried off so many and resolved to see the Elephant. Wood H. [Harvey] Helm and H. Copeland left friends and home for trip across the plains to the gold regions, which proved in the end

---

[75] *See* chapter 8. It is also barely possible that Prime came across the skull of the dead Indian that Israel Hale reported, who had asked a white man to shoot him in the head rather than be captured.

and to me, as in the case of so many, rather the nature of a wild
goose chase.[76]

Although it is important to honor the personal wishes of forty-niners,
this chapter will include only the most salient parts of Mr. Prime's eyewitness
account. He was someone who was truly a placer gold miner. Readers can
form their own ideas of what daily life was like for the actual participants in
what was America's greatest adventure. Prime wasn't a writer like some forty-
niners. Like Israel Hale and other miners, much of what he wrote was written
of necessity, in a hurry or when he was fatigued after working many hours of
hard physical labor. What stands out is his clarity and simplicity—good writing
qualities of any good piece of fiction, especially nonfiction.

In his first entry of March 18, 1850, he stated he left Linn in "Willworth
[Walworth] Co. Wisconsin for California with an ox team." He got underway by
progressing five miles. They "put up with Mr. Hutchinson on Big Foot Prune."[77]

After going another twenty miles, Prime noted they crossed "Stillman's
Creek and camped for night." After dining on some "fresh fish," their night
was broken up by having to pursue their cattle, which had "broke out of the
enclosure and took out the back track." It was an extremely cold night. They
"came near to freezing."[78]

The next few days were generally uneventful except for having to feed their
cattle on corn stalks because no hay was available. March 25 was somewhat
more eventful. Prime said he was "rather unwell."

> Before starting made a few alterations in our waggon [wagon] by
> fixing our waggon [wagon] cover, putting side irons on the box
> and a staple on the waggon [wagon] tongue. Drove to Sterling

---

[76] See Edward Prime, "Journal of Overland Journey, Wisconsin to San Francisco (by way
of the mines), Prospecting, Journey by Steamer, Train back to Wisc," Society of California
Pioneers Museum & Library, 101 Montgomery, S 150, The Presidio of San Francisco. This diary
is unnumbered, so all of the following footnotes in this chapter do not include page numbers.
Linn, Wisconsin, where Prime was from, is approximately sixty-three miles southeast of
Milwaukee in a rural region. Today, approximately two thousand residents live in Linn.
[77] *Ibid.*
[78] *Ibid.*

a handsome little village on the Rock River then five miles to Como also. On the Rock River. Liked the look of the country very much. During the day [?] and put up at Round Grove for the night. Felt rather unwell and took a horn of fourth proof [whiskey] which made one feel better (Accommodations were very good as we had a "clean floor" to sleep on).[79]

They passed through Council Bluffs, by Fort Laramie, and departed a little from the Oregon and California Trail to sightsee in Salt Lake City. There, Prime visited Kelly's Concert to satisfy his yearning for entertainment. On July 29, he was measured for a "pair of buckskin pants." The next day, his friend H. Copeland packed up his traps on his oxen because he'd grown too impatient to stay with Prime's party. On August 31, they drove five miles and camped on a small, unnamed creek. Prime described what happened next.

> There we found Shelby and Gibbs waiting for us. They having had enough of packing. At this place a number of persons were camped who had suffered more or less from the Indians. (They being very bad in this portion of country.) One man had two oxen stolen. Being half of his team. Another had two mules stolen. We appointed a strong guard (which was relieved in three hours)[80]

In spite of having some of Colonel Fremont's maps with them, they became lost on September 4. The stories they'd heard about "bad Indians" were confirmed by what happened the following day, September 5. Prime's terrible entire entry follows.

> After driving some two or three miles we came to a place where the ground was covered with blood for some distance around. An Indian's skull laid near with a ball hole in the back part of it. Two miles farther we found a piece of paper sticking into a

79 *Ibid.*

80 *Ibid.*

sage bush which had been written by a train some three days ahead of us. The paper stated that they had lain by at this place to bury two white men whom they found killed by the Indians. They also found one dead Indian near the body [bodies] of four more white men on the sides of the mountain near the road (Vengeance was sworn on every Indian that should make his appearance within rifle shot). The day twenty six miles and camped on a small creek with good feed and water rushing[,] sage brush for fuel.[81]

Another day passed with one more attack upon some Indians who had stolen five mules from Dr. Truett. One Indian was killed and several were probably injured. On September 11, they had to shoot one of their oxen for food. As they drove on, they discovered two fresh graves. One was a young man who'd grown up in Rock County, Wisconsin. Another was a white man shot in another fight with Indians. On September 12, they were involved in a fight with some Shoshone Indians, which ended in a draw. While it was still going on, fifty Mormons with one hundred head of horses arrived and were headed for Salt Lake City. They misinformed them that they had four hundred miles to go, which Prime found was a gross exaggeration. In actuality, California was much nearer.

Early in October, they arrived in Nevada City. They sold their stock. Prime's entry for October 12 reads,

> Sold off our stock (and was paid for our cattle in Feather River gold dust). Sold our cattle for seventy five dollars a yoke and the cow for seventy five dollars. Sold our wagon for twelve dollars (and got cheated awfully). Pitched our tent on Rock Creek and made preparations for mining.[82]

---

[81] *Ibid.*

[82] *Ibid.* Like many other immigrants to California, Prime noted that prices were higher once they arrived in California. He wasn't the only one who felt they were being cheated. However, their wagon may actually have been worth less in Nevada City because there might have been

After cleaning up, they went to Nevada City and bought provisions. The prices seemed exorbitant. "Pork fifty cents a pound. Fresh beef from twenty[-] five to thirty[.] Butter one dollar per pound.... And everything in proportion. We find it requires money to live here and a person without any has a poor show to get something to eat." On October 14, he added,

> Went to Nevada and bought some mining tools. Paid for a shovel
> ten dollars, for a pickaxe seven dollars, a rocker twenty dollars,
> wash pan two dollars and a half and every thing in proportion.[83]

During the next two weeks, he wrote a letter to "John." He sunk a shaft in three days to thirty feet, at which point water came in so quickly they had to quit. At last, on Deer Creek he made seven dollars and sixty-three cents. It was his first successful mining. He used a rocker on Deer Creek.

During the following week of early November 1850, he paid a Nevada City dentist sixteen dollars, spent one day in his camp reading, and found what he thought was a good prospective claim on the American River. On November 8, he was in Auburn, the future capital of Placer County. He would return there many times, almost always on a Sunday. It was a central point, a popular mining town where miners congregated to share their impressions, purchase provisions and tools, and meet other miners. On November 15, Prime noted,

> Made up our minds to leave the river. Crossed the river with our
> traps being two loads apiece and started for Pilot Hill. Camped
> on the side of the mountain. Had the <u>blues</u> awfully so to cure
> them got on a spree.[84]

This was one of the few times Mr. Prime admitted to drinking. Less than two weeks later, the seasonal California rain began in earnest on November 20. On November 22, they began building a "house ... We had to buck the

---

few, if any, buyers. Fortunately for Prime, and unlike most others, he must have brought enough cash with him to stake him for these early mining efforts.

[83] *Ibid.*

[84] *Ibid.*

framework a mile or more."[85] During the next four days, Prime and two others completed work on their house. They returned to prospecting "the ravine." His total for the first week in December was twenty-six dollars in gold. From December 17 through December 24, Prime's "company" of three men cleared a total of $65.90. On December 25, he noted, "Kept Christmas, Expenses $5.00."

On December 26, Prime recorded the facts about the murder of a miner named Avery and the subsequent pursuit of some Indians who may or may not have been guilty of the killing. From the tone, it doesn't appear that Prime personally played any active role other than being an observer. His journal entries from December 26–28, are included below.

Dec. 26

There is quite an excitement among the miners this morning occasioned by the disappearance of a young miner by the name of Avery supposed to be shot by the Indians. A company of one hundred and fifty men were soon raised and started out in search of him. Going four miles came to an (Indian rancho) soon as they saw the whites (Excepting four who were taken prisoners[.]) They had Avery's rifle. Took them to Pilot Hill calculating to investigate the matter as soon as possible[.] (Put them under guard[.])

Dec. 27

One of the Indians was shot this morning (in attempting to escape[.]) from the guards.

Dec. 28

Had an examination of the prisoners who were found guilty and two of them were hung accordingly, the third was kept to show us where the body of Avery was hid. Sent to Coloma for

---

85 *Ibid.*

an Indian interpreter as there was no one who understood the language of the tribe.

Dec. 29

Very pleasant. Found on questioning the Indian (by the interpreter} where the body of Avery was secreted. Went about a mile north east [northeast] of town and found him buried under an old rotten log and covered

With leaves (the place had all the appearance of not having been disturbed for years) His body had eight arrow holes through it and otherwise very much mutilated. Took the body in town and burned [buried] it. Likewise hung the remaining Indian of the same tribe with the rest[.][86]

It appears possible that Prime may have been part of the party that followed up using the interpreter's information as to the location of Avery's body. One reason this seems likely is that his description on December 29 was so specific as to the facts of the appearance of the place where Mr. Avery's body was found.

This very sad incident affected him, apparently quite deeply, because it took him almost a full week before he returned to work. Then he made five dollars. From January 2–4 he "had a fit of the blues," so there was no mining. On January 6, 1851, his journal states that he used a rocker. We can safely assume he was in camp. He continued mining in the Pilot Hill region until February 4, when they decided to call it quits and to move on after making a total of only just thirty-eight dollars.

Prime, along with three coworkers, walked to Illinoistown and then to Nevada on February 6. Although he certainly wasn't getting rich at mining,

---

[86] *Ibid.* Again, by current standards of crime investigation, the whites' actions in this case seem cruelly unfair. At the very least, they were hasty. However, we need to remember that standards of justice in the California mining regions in 1850 were far more primitive and racially biased.

Prime found the prospects of making a rich gold strike interesting. What sustained Prime, as well as most other forty-niners, was the camaraderie he felt with his coworkers and other miners. On February 6, he wrote, "At Nevada City found some old acquaintances of the plains."[87]

It was so rainy during the spring of 1851 that he and his companions didn't accomplish much in the way of mining.

Jumping ahead to May 14, after noting they worked hard in passing through snow banks, which varied from "five to fifteen feet in depth," he noted being in the company of "women prospectors" two days before.

> Got in company with women prospecters [prospectors] from Feather River who was return [were returning] to Downieville (with some success as ourselves)[.] We traveled twenty five miles over creeks and mountains and through dense chaparell [chapparel] until we were "used up men." We arrived in camp about dark with our clothes in strings and our hands and faces covered with blood (occasioned by the thorny chaparell). Had a good supper we stood in need of.[88]

After being at work in a thirty-foot-deep shaft on the fifteenth, Prime worked two of the next three days. On May 19 he noted, "While at work was taken with an attack of the paralysis."[89] Possibly aided by coworkers, he then "went to Downieville after medication."

Taking the next day to rest in bed—"Was my own physician"—he was too sick (and also perhaps too depressed) to work until May 26. He noted,

> Worked a little but was a more fit subject for my bed than washing gold. Van returned from a prospecting tour (having been out three or four days).[90]

---

[87] Ibid.

[88] *Ibid.*

[89] *Ibid.*, What Prime described here as "paralysis" was common among many other forty-niners. Some physicians or nurses today might call this "seizures" but it may have simply been due to stress and overwork.

[90] *Ibid.*

He returned with his coworker Van to using their rocker and earned $18.50 for the next four days. They were not making enough even to break even. As May came to an end, Prime and his company decided to take their traps and move to another location "down the Yuba." On June 2 they were taking up claims on Spencer's Bar.

On June 7–9 he made a trip to Downieville and back to Spencer's Bar to buy some hose. By this time, having had about six months at work at mining, Prime may have guessed that he probably would not strike it rich. Nevertheless, he sensed that if he kept at it, he could more than just break even. On June 11, he "bought 130 yards more of hose." They needed the hose to bring water close to their claims "for washing."[91] On June 13, he "laid 480 feet of hose." Two days later, he spent four dollars for Epsom salts from Dr. Arnold. Over the next six days, they made thirty-six dollars in gold. Because there were two of them at work, his take-home pay was just eighteen dollars.

Through much of the summer of 1851, Prime continued working claims he and his partner, Van, had made on Spencer's Bar, only just scraping by. In August they moved to a new site on the Yuba River, where he continued to only get by. Starting in September, now with his partners Alva, Oren, and Van, Prime had slightly more encouraging results.

Sept. 1

> In company with Van, Oren and Alvah Gow took up some claims
> on a little bar in the river. Dug a small race to carry off the
> surface water and commenced washing with the rocker about
> ten o'clock and made during the day 110.00.[92]

Prime didn't make a single dollar sign after amounts made daily throughout his journal because he wrote it for his own use or his family's eventual reference. One has the feeling throughout that he was only interested in recording bare facts, not his reactions to events or his feelings or those of

---

[91] *Ibid.*
[92] Ibid.

fellow miners. The following day's entry read "Ditto" to the left and "216.00" on the right side.

As the month of September passed, Prime noted that their total for the following ten days including September 13 was $256. It was his most profitable time in the mines so far.

Something unusual occurred on the night of September 15 in Auburn.

Sept.15

> Left the Yuba River for Auburn, night at the Hayville House. We were disturbed about twelve o'clock by four suspicious looking fellows from a Negro Tent (who were armed to the teeth). They staid [stayed] the remainder of the day (and the night following).[93]

Prime said nothing else about the four "suspicious" (to him) characters, who were well armed. Probably they appeared to the white men to be potentially dangerous. How the white men appeared to the blacks was unnoted. Perhaps the four men were in a room near where Prime and his party were, and the noise of their arrival awoke them.

During the remainder of 1851, Prime's journal reflected a satisfied miner who could take off some time. On September 17, he walked to Nevada City, where he ran into "Harvey and Jim Wood," who had gone across the plains with Prime. Soon after, they began to work on claims made on Spanish Ravine. After a short visit to Sacramento, where he encountered "a number of old friends," Prime returned to Auburn. There, on September 27 he noted, "Shaved and had my haircut (for the first time in eighteen months)." Unlike young people today the forty-niners had little time for civilized niceties of even the most basic kind like haircuts or shaves. Two days later, he was back to work again at Spanish and Auburn ravines. This work continued with no result through early October.

On October 26, along with his associate Van, he took a stage to Sacramento, where he spent the evening of October 27 at the American Theater. The next

---

[93] *Ibid.* It is also probable that the four African American armed men would have been alarming to Prime, who, having been born and raised in Wisconsin, may never have had any direct contact with blacks.

day, he returned by stage to Auburn. While he continued to prospect at a few locations like Baltimore Ravine (October 29–30) and Cold Spring Creek near Coloma on December 11, he didn't find any rich claims. It was back to Auburn by way of Hangtown where he stayed at Washington House. He returned to Auburn on December 15, traveling a total of thirty-eight miles. He stated he had "done but little" during the period from December 16–31 but "Prospected some in the big ravine."[94]

The year 1852 in the mines for Edward Prime began with some moderate success. On January 2 and 3, he "Worked our claims and took out 20.00 [dollars' worth of gold]." Two acquaintances, "John & Steve," arrived in Auburn the following day but decided against staying at the Florence Saloon because there had been "a number of small pox" cases there. During the next six days, Prime and his partner Van "washed from our claims .... 100.00."[95] By January 24, they had added $50.80. He took another break and apparently went back to Auburn, where on January 25 he wrote, "Received four letters and paid 9.50 postage."[96]

After that date, he began to "mess" [formed a company with] Van, Steve, John, and Hank Caster at a log cabin on the Spanish Ravine. He wrote, "Feb, 2, 3, 4, 5, 6, 7 Made apiece the last week 27.40." For the next week, February 15–21, they "made apiece 16.75." And for the next week, the company of five cleared $145 ($29.00 apiece).

As he had a number of times before, Prime took a break from mining. Along with Steve, he left Auburn "for the Yuba" on February 23, heading for Nevada City. They stayed at Empire, where he saw "J. Wood and Harvey Helm." Helm was his first companion on the trail across the plains the previous year.

After making a rough trip back to his claims, Prime got down to working in earnest during the summer. His company built a flume as well as stringers to assist with their manual labor. From September 11 to October 16, 1852, his journal entries totaled $4,075.60, no doubt requiring at least some form of

---

94 *Ibid.*

95 *Ibid.*

96 *Ibid.* The practice of paying for stamps and affixing them to envelopes was not in general use in the United States before it was adopted here in the late1850s. More than ten years before this, in 1840, Sir Roland Hill had invented the penny post in England. Before that, the addressee paid the letter carrier the postage due.

a "Eureka!"[97] "Oct. 17 Received from Chinamen 207.20."[98] There was nothing about why. The same entry made it clear they were not succeeding: "Settled up and found (after paying up our liabilities) that we were 'minus.'"

Clearly, their luck had run out. Their claims were "played out." From October 18 to November 4, he explained, "Worked on our claims for the last eighteen days and did not make expenses. Discharged all of our hired help."[99] On November 5, he "gave up my interest in the claims (and left for Downieville)."

After visiting Downieville and Nevada City, he wrote this entry on November 13.

> Left Auburn and went down to Secrest [Secret]
>
> Diggins where I found Van and John mining (Likewise a number more of the boys). [100]

After obtaining a third partner, "Dan C.," from "Nov. 15–30–Dec. 1–31 left our boarding house at (Old Pikes) and commenced boarding ourselves." California's rainy season had set in, so it wasn't possible to accomplish much in the way of digging.

In 1853 the gold diggings began. Describing the period from January 2–31, Prime wrote, "In company with Tom Leonard worked sinking shaft on Shugar [Sugar] Loaf Hill (excepting rainy weather)." In the next entry, February 1–12, Prime noted, "Finished our shaft (which was sixty-]two feet deep and found nothing to pay." Discouraged, he left "Secreet Diggins in company with Dan & T. Leonard for the North having been at Secreet Diggins since Nov. 13th and not made board." The next location he moved to was the North Yuba River area on February 18. After building a cabin, he returned to prospecting on November 23 and 24. The following day, probably with his associates, he "made a boat to cross the river."[101] Beginning in the fall, this boat turned out to be one

---

97 *Ibid.*

98 *Ibid.*

99 *Ibid.*

100 *Ibid.*

101 *Ibid.*

his most valuable investments. On February 28, Dan C. Prime and Tom began digging a tunnel "in a flat on the bank of the river," but after about two weeks, they stopped due to a lack of funds. After working four days at "tunneling," he "washed out 17.00." Working the same way, he noted on March 11 they had made "21.00." Then from February 12 to 31 he wrote, "Left off tunneling for the want of funds to carry it on."[102]

On April 1, he briefly separated from Dan C. and Tom Leonard to become Jim Hartwell's partner. Between April 5 and April 15, Prime and Hartwell removed ninety-seven dollars' worth of gold working with a Long Tom despite heavy rains.

They were working as hard as they possibly could, but their results weren't very great. Prime noted next how important the local banks were to the miners. "April 16–22 Made nothing of importance in the last week as (our banks) suspended payments and storming most of the time." After stopping off briefly at Oak Valley and Oregon Creek with their traps, he went back to Downieville and did a little more prospecting at Oak Valley until May 14. In the following entry, Mr. Prime realized that despite all his best efforts, he wasn't clearing enough to live on, so, "May 15–2[,] Worked for Cowen at four dollars per day digging a water ditch[.]"[103]

It was a tough time for him because digging gold wasn't paying well—certainly not as he well as he had hoped or even as it once had been. In early June, he was "cutting hay for Old Pike at four dollars and a half a day." He had begun working for other mining outfits throughout the summer.

At last, on October 20 he committed himself, along with doubtlessly much of his own money, "In company with O. S. Grow and H. Custer bought out the company at Yankee Slide at the foot of Connecticut Bar on the North Fork of the American River (and took possession of the slide and ferry)."[104] After working hard through October and the first nine days of November, they began washing out gold. On November 10, it amounted to eleven dollars. His prospects had begun to improve a bit, although the results were steady throughout the fall and winter of 1853. By December 26, it amounted to $255.29, which was a

---

[102] *Ibid.*

[103] *Ibid.*

[104] *Ibid.*

modest yet steady income. This included twelve dollars "made by ferry" during the same period.

He was making just enough through working the American River claim and the ferry to remain at it. The year 1853 came to an end with Prime noting they made a total of $32.75.

Edward Prime's final year at work digging for gold in Northern California was 1854. He wasn't destined to achieve great wealth in his time in the gold fields, yet he may well have achieved more in terms of true happiness there than he did later in life.

The amounts he posted in his diary early in the year were not much different than those he listed at the end of 1853. During the first week of 1854, his company's mining was a total of $52.85, and for the ferrying it was $4.50. At this point, he was also making bimonthly payments "on our account to Parkerson," a total of $206.16 during January. Rainy weather prevented them from making more, but on some of those days, they worked repairing their equipment, such as a Long Tom, a rocker, sluice boxes, and a water wheel. Prime was the member of the company who went to Auburn to make the company's payments (which must have been on a loan). In the meantime, during January they "washed out: a total of two hundred fifty-six dollars."[105]

Interestingly, he recorded on January 12 that it "rained hard all day." Furthermore, on the thirteenth, "Still rainy the river rises very fast. The water is thirty feet higher than low water mark. Floome [flume] and all kinds of lumber coming down the river."[106] This note possibly gave him the idea on which they later (May 29) capitalized. This idea was to chop timber, which they floated on rafts down the American River and sold in Sacramento.

Returning to his diary on February 1–3, he noted, "Waiting for rain. Went hunting," but he did not record if they bagged anything. On the following day, he reported what they had made "with the ferry in the past week ... 29.50."[107] On March 8, his company of three miners increased by two to five as "Van and

---

[105] *Ibid.*

[106] *Ibid.*

[107] *Ibid.*

Alvah" joined the "mess."[108] It was funds earned by the ferry that tided them over during the next ten days because the heavy snow and rain of the season prevented them from doing much mining. The total for two weeks of manning their ferry was $97.88. Added to this was "46.75" on March 25.

While they "commenced running another drift into Yankee Slide" on March 27, they had no mining results before the first week of April. Sensing their lack of funds might well continue, Prime noted on March 29, "Bought some seed and made a garden for our special use." On March 31, Prime made another trip to Auburn

> to witness the execution of Robt. Scott who was executed for the murder of Andrew King. At an early hour the streets of Auburn were crowded with spectators. It was estimated that there was [were] five to eight thousand persons at the execution. Good order prevailed throughout the day. On the scaffold he stated that his[109] name was not Robert Scott (which was a fictitious name). His reasons for not giving his true name were that he had a father and mother living and did not wish them to know what had become of him.

> Staid [stayed] in town all day. Received a letter from home.[110]

Like two and a half years earlier, in the case of Avery's murder involving Indians, after it was over, Prime made no further note of it in his journal. On April 1, he noted they had made "by the ferry during the past week, 55.00 and 35.25." Late in March, they constructed a "car" to help carry dirt. Despite the fact that they weren't finding much gold, he took time away from their claims to go to "the Calf. Bar ... to see the boys" (April 9) and to go to Auburn (April

---

[108] *Ibid.* Other miners also used the term mess. The US military, then and now, sometimes uses mess to mean a serviceperson is included, as when a unit sits down together for meals in a mess hall.

[109] *Ibid.*

[110] *Ibid.*

10). "Saw Dan. At Auburn on his way for home. (Went to Lee and Marshall's Circus in the evening)."[111]

Like some others, Dan had had his fill of the search for the always elusive California gold. Still, two days later, Prime recorded making "20.50" in gold.

Although there was only one entry for gold of "3.00" during the following week of April, on April 15 and April 22, their ferry business cleared a total of $45.50. Their production of gold rose a bit by much washing and using their rocker; they totaled $489 on May 20. During the same three weeks, they earned a total of $63.00 by ferrying miners across the American River. Mr. Prime's patience with mining was running thin, so much so that on May 27, he wrote, "Got the blues. Paid off the comp. [company, or part-time laborers?]." Prime added, "Made by the ferry during the past week 17.50."[112]

On May 29, "Got tired of mining and entered into partnership with four other persons to raft timber down the American River to Sacramento City." Like many others, Prime was turning to a secondary way of making a living in northern California. The next day, he started "getting out the timber," and on June 1, "Left Auburn by the stage at 7 o'clock A.M. The rest of the boys staid [stayed] to raft the timber down the river. (Went to Sacramento to find sale for our timber.)"[113] He spent the next three days in Sacramento, where he saw "Me," whom he had dinner with the first evening, and later "J. Lewis." On June 5, he went upriver to meet his partners camping on the river bank near Mormon Island. On the sixth, he met the others "four miles above Mormon Island" and worked all day helping them with "the rafting." It was "tedious business." He returned to Sacramento and "roved about the city with A.V.B." from June 10 to June 18. He returned to camp on June 19. "Got back to camp and found we had made by our timber speculation about $100 apiece over the left."[114]

---

[111] *Ibid.*

[112] *Ibid.*

[113] Ibid.

[114] *Ibid.* The phrase "over the left" was a common nineteenth-century colloquialism that meant "surprisingly" or "unexpectedly." Literally, it meant "over the left shoulder." If a child seemed to be left-handed, it was common for schoolteachers to tie his or her arm to force the child to use only its right arm, to make it dominant. Many held that to be left-handed meant the person was "wrong-handed."

While he was in Sacramento, his partners had worked the ferry to make
$65.00. He was back at work "on our claims" from June 21 to June 26, making a
total of $17.50, except for a Sunday in Auburn on June 25. During the following
week, he did nothing and was in camp. The only break in his monotony was
getting "a letter from home" on July 2. On July 7, he "worked for Udall at Calf.
Bar." On July 19, he

> commenced laying wall for our wing dam (Three in Company)-.=
> Had to lay the wall in the water (which was cold as ice)[.][115]

During the next two days, he continued to lay wall. On June 13, he "hired
two Chinamen to help us in our apperations [operations]." They were all
working hard through the rest of July. On July 17 he added, "Still working in
the water laying wall. Had to use plenty of the <u>ardent</u> to keep our blood in
circulation."[116] On July 24 he wrote, "Still laying wall for wing [written in above
by Mr. Prime is 'dam']." They continued their work. On July 29, he added, "Paid
chinamen forty-five dollars."[117]

On August 1 he wrote, "Finished the dam having been to work in the water
for the last twenty days. The water was deep and cold with a heavy current." It
was difficult, painstaking manual labor for which they suffered. Many miners
fell ill. Some died from scurvy and pneumonia. On August 3, Prime wrote,
"Rigging the pumps to take the water out of the claims."[118] They put their water
wheel into use. On August 5 he recorded, "Rigged up for washing the comeing

---

[115] *Ibid.*

[116] *Ibid.* It's unknown what Mr. Prime meant by ardent. Perhaps it was whiskey or more likely
brandy.

[117] *Ibid.* This was Prime's first mention of the Chinese, who definitely were a large part of the
California Gold Rush. Some of them took what they had earned mining back to China, whereas
others remained in California and settled in towns and cities across the state. *Chinamen* was a
pejorative term used by many whites for generations, and it's definitely unacceptable today.
In many cases, the Chinese immigrants gained some productive claims when white miners'
patience ran out, selling off their claims to either move on or to "see the elephant" and give up.

[118] *Ibid.*

[coming] week. Got our long tom sluice boxes etc." He had to go to Auburn on August 6 "after provisions."[119]

Then, as he returned to work, he reported on August 7, "Commenced washing with the long tom on our claims. Hired two chinamen who we paid three dollars per day. Took out of the claims 150.00."[120]

Their hard work since June to get their claims ready began to pay. The amount removed from Yankee Slide from August 8 to August 19 was $1,122. On that same date, he recorded, "Our expenses for hired men during the past week amounted to one hundred fifty dollars."[121] From August 20 through August 25, they removed another $173 in gold.

Prime went to Auburn on the twenty-sixth. Their "company expenses" were slightly more, at $174.25, than they made in the last five days. On August 29 he "built a head dam across the upper end of the claims." On August 30, he

> made a foot dam and put the pump in operation. Prospected and found the river had been previously worked. Discharged most of our hired hands as we found it would not pay to keep them.[122]

Aside from a trip to Auburn for provisions, from August 31 through September 5, they brought out $224 in gold using the Long Tom and washing. On September 2, he noted their expenses had been $167 for the previous week. Prime did his civic duty on September 6 as he "attended election Calf. Bar."

Despite their getting a small amount on September 12, Prime and his partners "made up our minds to leave California and start for home." He also stated on the same day that he "sold out our claims to a gang of Chinamen for seventy-five dollars."[123] Seemingly, it was a sudden move. They spent September 13 "selling off company property consisting of water wheels, pumps, long toms and tools of every description for mining purposes."[124] On September 19, he

---

[119] *Ibid.*

[120] *Ibid.*

[121] For brevity purposes, I have taken the liberty to total up a number of days' earnings at several points in this chapter and in later chapters of this book.

[122] *Ibid.*

[123] *Ibid.*

[124] *Ibid.*

repeated that they "sold out our claims in Yankee slide to a company of (Hong Kong)." On September 21, he wrote,

> Bid farewell to all our friends at Auburn not knowing when or where ("if ever") we should meet again. Received the kind congratulations of all and took our seats in the stage for Sacramento City. Arrived at Sacramento at 2 o'clock P.M. Put up at the U.S. Hotel.[125]

The following day in Sacramento, he visited friends Will McDougall and J. W. Lewis. The next day, he took the four o'clock boat to San Francisco, where he stayed at the Essex House for the night. On September 24, he "called on Mabe. Lymenson at 82 Comercial [Commercial] St. Roved about the city most of the day. Went to hear the Backus [Bacchus][126] Theater in the evening." On September 25 he "saw Capt. Nye. Went to the Assaying Office and had our dust assayed which yielded seventeen dollars and eighty-four cents an ounce."[127]

"Went to the Metropolitan Theater in the evening." On September 26, he crossed San Francisco Bay, walking "to Alvarado." In the San Jose Valley, he met with two friends "John and Steve," who were "threshing." On September 27, he caught a stage to Oakland and returned to San Francisco "at noon."[128]

On September 28, he bought a steamship ticket at the Nicaragua Steamship Company office. The next day, he "called on C. French, T. Richardber, Flint, and Welch likewise a number of Canajoharie[?] friends."[129] The advertised date to depart San Francisco was September 30, but

> For the sailing of the three Steamers *Yankee Blade*, *Cortes* and *Sonora*[.] The streets were crowded with people of all classes

---

[125] *Ibid.*

[126] Bacchus was the Greek god of wine.

[127] Although the generally accepted price of gold was twenty-six dollars per ounce at the mint, it would appear that Prime only got about 69 percent of what his gold was actually worth. Most miners in San Francisco weren't in a position to question it, especially if, like Prime was, they were

[128] *Ibid.*

[129] Ibid.

hurrying to and fro as if they were on business of life or death, The Steamers *Cortes* and *Yankee Blade* lay opposite each other at the foot of the Pacific St. Wharf. While the *Sonora* lay moored at Valejo St. wharf. As the time approached for leaving the crowd (on the wharf) became so dense that it was almost impossible to pass. Adieus and congratulations were exchanged between the passengers and their friends ashore. At four o'clock P.M. the three steamers left their moorings and started down the Bay. The *Yankee Blade* taking the lead while the *Cortes* followed in her wake and last (though not least) came the *Sonora*. As each boat left the wharf a salute of three guns was fired. Which was answered by three cheers from the crowd on shore, About 6 P.M. the weather became so foggy and cold that it was disagreeable to stay on deck so went below and turned in for the night (With the consolation that I was homeward bound).[130]

In spite of some "stormy" weather (especially near the end of the voyage) and a lack of pure water, thirteen days later, on October 13, the *Cortes* "arrived at the harbor of San Juan/Del Sur and anchored." The passengers were rowed to land for the price of one dollar per person. It was only a twelve-mile journey by mules across Nicaragua, although the four hundred people who made the trip with Prime also had to cross Lake Nicaragua. On October 14 ne noted,

At 5 o'clock in the morning we were across Lake Nicaragua and began to descend the River of San Juan. Went down the river twelve miles and arrived at Castille where we again changed steamers ... on account of the river being very shallow. Arrived a San Juan Del Norte two o'clock A.M. While passing down the river of San Juan we saw a number of large alligators along the

---

[130] Ibid. Prime was a passenger on the *Cortes*. Approximate distance from San Francisco to San Juan del Sur, Nicaragua, is 4,583 kilometers. The approximate distance from San Francisco to Panama is 5,350 kilometers. There might have been less threat of becoming ill crossing Nicaragua versus crossing Panama.

banks, also plenty of monkeys at our approach making the air resound with their howling and screeching.[131]

On October 15, by sunrise they were "all on board of the steamship *Star of the West* which lay anchored in sight of Greytown. At twelve A.M. set sail for New York with a beauiful [beautiful] breeze flowing from N. West."

Oct. 16

Very pleasant. On taking observation found we had made 290 miles since leaving Del Norte. Weather very warm which makes it rather uncomfortable sleeping below. Promenaded the deck until a late hour at night (enjoying a moonlight scene on the bosom of the ocean). The spray (as it dashed from the bows of our gallent craft). Looked as if we were passing through an innumerable multitude of fire-flies while far down (apparently) in the blue depths of the ocean the heavens were reflected as in a mirror.[132]

The first three days at sea were warm, blissful sailing. However, things suddenly changed on October 19 as the ship approached Key West putting in for a load of coal for their trip up the eastern seaboard to New York. A recent yellow fever epidemic had "left ... the greater portion of the city ... nearly desolate." He went ashore on the nineteenth, noting the "curiosities of the place until a late hour when we retired to our humble cots."[133] The ship departed early on the twentieth and soon ran into stormy weather with extremely rough seas. He was seasick. On October 22, they "left the Gulf Stream. At night ran a very narrow chance of being shipwrecked on a shoal of rocks." There is no additional explanation as to why or where they were when he noted this.

The next day off Cape Hattaras, the "ocean very rough." Prime and "a great many others" could not leave their staterooms due to seasickness. On October 24, as the *Star of West* went into Norfolk, Virginia, for coal, he "roamed about

---

[131] *Ibid.*

[132] *Ibid.*

[133] *Ibid.*

the City until a late hour at night. <u>Taking items and eating oysters</u> (Virginia hospital [hospitality] City will beat the world)."[134] On October 27, they arrived in New York. He "put up at the Lovejoy Hotel." During the night, he got so suddenly sick that he had to call for a doctor (whose kind care) I cannot forget."[135]

Unless possibly in contact through the telegraph, or perhaps by an earlier letter to them, it is a mystery how Prime's old friends learned that he was about to land in New York, On October 28 he wrote,

> Some of my old friends (and school mates) came to see me which brought back to me [my] memory the scenes of bygone days (transacted in the old school) when we were boys together. By inquiry I found that of all the boys who were school mates then but few remained near the spot where our boyhood days had been squandered. Some have met on the distant lands of California but many have gone to the long home from whence no traveler [traveler] returns (Sad thought). A change in my sickness (for the better) commenced at eight in the morning. In the afternoon was able to set up for a short time although still in great distress. In the evening in company with J. Putnam and Marsh went to hear the Christie Minstrels (although I was more fit substitute for bed) and was far from being well.[136]

Premature death was much more common 170 years ago because medicine has made so many advances, and education levels have brought us greater abilities to care for ourselves. Mr. Prime convalesced for the next two days, although he was well enough on October 30 to "go to Barnum in the afternoon and the Broadway Theater in the evening (in company with Putnam)."[137]

He left New York on the steamer *Isaac Newton* at 6:00 p.m. He arrived in Albany at 4:00 a.m. on November 2. Leaving Albany two hours later by train, he reached Syracuse at four o'clock "(on the lightning train) and arrived in Buffalo

---

[134] *Ibid.*

[135] *Ibid.*

[136] *Ibid.*

[137] *Ibid.*

at eight in the evening."[138] On November 5, he arrived in Chicago after a ride on the Central Michigan Railroad. His arrival home (probably Linn, Wisconsin, or possibly Geneva, Wisconsin) completed his journal, except for eight later entries mentioning friends and family members he visited in November 1854. His entry for November 6 was,

> Got up this morning (with the consolation) that I was again near home. Met many familiar countainances [countenances]. Parted company with my old friend (and partner) [either Harvey Helm or H. Copeland] of Calafornia [California] scenes and left for home with my parents whom I was very glad to see once more, and so ends my long and tedious journey to & from Calafornia [California][.] Called on Mary & Aunt Weaver[;] from there went over to ("Old joe's") and met Mary (The scene was that of the Prodigal Brother) son.[139]

Two days later, he mentioned he saw "Uncle Ehles." On November 9 he visited George C. Hellen and Mr. Turner. On the tenth he revisited "Aunt Weaver" and "called on Netty." On November 11, Prime "called at Daniel L. Cornues." On November 12, he "went to meeting at the Gravel school house." On the thirteenth, he "went to see Mr. and Mrs. Phillips." The final entry to his journal was on November 14. "Went over to see my old friend Nate. Visited with Henry and Rowena."[140]

Author's Note

Several facts are obvious about Mr. Prime's journal. Almost certainly Prime was a young man because nobody who wasn't young and healthy could have survived his experiences as a gold miner in the California Gold Rush of the early 1850s. Although his journal was painstakingly done with almost daily entries,

---

[138] Ibid. It's interesting to note that passenger train travel in the east by the 1850s was efficient and speedy.

[139] *Ibid.* Because he compared himself to the Prodigal Son, Mary probably was either his mother or a sister.

[140] *Ibid.*

Prime neglected to tell the reader of the total amount he was personally able to keep or how much was the company's share. In other words, was the amount completely his, or did he split it up two or more ways depending on how many miners comprised the company at any given time? We may never know the answer.

A second area of mystery is where and when Edward Prime was born. Although his journal included notes he wrote during his trip to Pike's Peak after all the notes on California, there are apparently no death or marriage records of him from his later life in the records; I've checked at the Wisconsin State Historical Society online. He appears to vanish following this later journey. There is no record of him to show whether he remained in Wisconsin; he could have moved elsewhere.

The bound diary is a transcription that was donated to the Society of California Pioneers by Miss Ethel Haran.

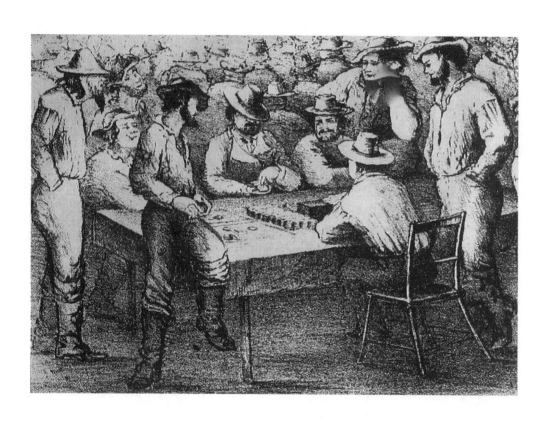

MINERS

CHAPTER 5

James Delavan and Samuel McNeil

I saw three men dig our $9000 in seven days, and two men dig $2500 in two days. But these are rare circumstances. I saw a Spaniard having a lump of gold he had found weighing one pound and a half.

—Samuel McNeil, Stanish Lou diggings, 1849

It was the mid-nineteenth century. If anyone wanted to prospect for and mine California gold, first he or she had to get to this remote region. This wasn't quick or easy, as it would be today. The route around Cape Horn took the longest, until clipper ships considerably shortened the time. The next longest was cross-country. One might take another ship to the east coast of Panama, Chagres; cross the Isthmus; and sail north from Panama up to San Francisco. Thirdly, one might cross the American Great Plains by wagon train and scale the Rocky Mountains and the Sierra Nevada to arrive from the east. Or one could take a sailing ship to the east coast of Nicaragua, cross it, and sail up the West Coast to San Francisco—probably the shortest in length and taking the least time. Lastly, one could reach New Orleans by land or down the Mississippi River, sail to northeastern Mexico or Texas, ride a mule across northern Mexico to Mazatlan, and sail north to San Francisco. As already seen with the account of Edward Prime, and as we will see below with the account of Israel Hale, some chose the overland route. An excerpt from the *California Star* read,

> Every seaport as far south as San Diego, and every interior town, and nearly every rancho from the base of the mountains in which the gold has been found, to the Mission of San Luis, south, has become suddenly drained of human beings. Americans, Californians, Indians and Sandwich Islanders, men, women and

children, indiscriminately. Should there be that success which has repaid the efforts of those employed for the last month, during the present and next, as many are sanguine in their expectations, and we confess to unhesitatingly believe probably, not only will witness the depopulation of every town, the desertion of every rancho, and the desolation of the once promising crops of the country, but it will also draw largely upon adjacent territories—awake Sonora, and call down upon us, despite her Indian battles, a great many of the good people of Oregon.

Due to coming down with an illness or being attacked by Indians, traveling entirely overland was the most dangerous. One gold-seeker, on the Oregon Trail in 1852,[141] counted six graves of dead emigrants for each mile traveled between Missouri and Fort Laramie.

James Delavan had no family connections or other possible advantages when he began thinking of making the voyage to California. It was December 1848, and after reading the report to President Polk by Captain Richard Mason and numerous newspaper articles, Delavan and thousands of others readily learned some of the incredible facts about the richness of the gold fields of California.

The two forty-niners in this chapter had little in common except for the fact they spent only a few months in California and published travelogues or guides meant to inform others planning travel to California to try their hand at gold mining. Delavan was no longer a youth but had not yet reached middle age. Because it was winter on the East Coast, the wrong time of year for crossing the Great Plains, he immediately ruled out crossing the continent by land. Instead, he chose the second route from the earlier list: sailing to Panama and crossing the Isthmus, because it was "the shortest by land." He added to his diary, "I determined to embark for the Bay of Darien, and go by way of the Isthmus of Panama, and thence up the coast to St. [San] Francisco."[142] His steerage ticket on

---

[141] Dr. John Hudson Wayman. See *A Doctor on the California Trail: The Diary of Dr. John Hudson Wayman, 1852*, ed. Edgeley Woodman Todd (Denver: The Old West Publishing Company, 1971).
[142] James Delavan, *Notes on California and the Placers How to Get There, and What to Do Afterwards*, foreword by Joseph A. Sullivan (Oakland, CA: Biobooks, 1956), 3. Delavan's travelogue was originally published in 1850.

board the passenger ship, *Falcon,* cost $150. To be sure that he'd have necessary provisions once he arrived in California, he sent a supply on board the *Brooklyn,* which would sail around Cape Horn.

A crewman ushered him around the *Falcon,* and he was shown a cabin. However, once aboard, and after the ship had left port, he found his berth wound up to be in steerage, packed in with others in a small space, with only a cot on which to sleep. After a trip across the Gulf of Mexico, on the morning of February 12, 1849, the ship arrived at Chagres. Despite a pouring rain, the captain, Captain Thompson, wasted no time in clearing the ship of passengers because he knew his pay depended on keeping his ship filled with returning passengers to the States.

A committee of gold seekers formed to negotiate with the owners of the *Orus,* a Panamanian steamer, to take them partway across the isthmus to the town of Panama, on the west coast of the isthmus. As another ship, the *Crescent City,* arrived in Chagres just after the *Falcon,* suddenly there were fifteen hundred adventurers, each one trying to be the first to cross the isthmus. It soon became clear to Delavan that only by hiring a native to carry his baggage on his back could he reach Panama with what he'd need later, once he finally arrived in San Francisco. Delavan wisely took a week off at Chagres before doing anything.

During the same month, February 1849, when James Delavan reached the east coast of Panama, another gold fever patient, a Midwestern shoemaker named Samuel McNeil, joined a newly formed party of adventurers, totaling eleven including him, in central Ohio. McNeil hailed from the town of Lancaster, located a little more than thirty miles southwest of Columbus. McNeil was happily married to his childhood friend, partner, and sweetheart, Ellen. The couple had several young children. Both he and Ellen realized the very large risk he was taking. McNeill was one of thousands deeply taken by the virulent epidemic known as gold fever. The party included Boyd Ewing, the son of the secretary of the interior; an honest constable; and others from other professions. It included a clever lawyer, named Stambaugh. Even before he joined the company of gold seekers, other members of his party who knew McNeill didn't think much of him. As it turned out, McNeil managed to find a good niche for himself in California, making a steady income while most of the others were failures. Other members of his party didn't do nearly as well as he did. Later, in 1850, having already returned to Columbus, the shoemaker-turned-tavern-owner published his memoir about his California experiences, a popular guide to other prospective emigrants entitled *McNeil's Travels in 1849 to, throughout, and from the Gold Regions, in California.*

Once he braced himself to travel in the tropical heat of the Isthmus, Delavan hired a native "peon," as he called him, to carry his luggage in the hot sun. It was a dangerous passage that left many forty-niners dead or in poor health from snakebite, malaria, yellow fever, or cholera. In March, Delavan arrived in Panama to find the town was "filled to overflowing with pilgrims of hope."[143] It was vital to get a berth on board the passenger ship *Oregon;* if he failed, he might have languished in Panama for months until another steamer arrived. Delavan took the time to describe some of his fellow gold seekers.

> And to see them armed to the teeth, rifle in hand, many with two pistols and a knife hanging from their belts, one would have supposed that they expected to encounter at every step, some hydra-headed monster.[144]

Paying from three hundred to four hundred dollars apiece for a ticket, passengers still were not home free from Panama. Travelers also paid up to two dollars each to hire what was called a "bungo," another native with a skiff, to row them one by one with their baggage out to the ship, which was anchored in the harbor. After taking over a month to cross the isthmus, on March 13, 1849, Delavan and the other passengers were relieved when the steamer *Oregon* raised its anchor and sailed out into the Pacific Ocean. It traveled northward rapidly with the assistance of helpful currents and favorable winds, and just over two weeks later, the *Oregon* arrived in San Francisco on April 1, 1849. Aware that San Francisco was California's primary seaport, Delavan decided to spend ten days there. His description is well worth recording.

---

[143] *Ibid.,* 20.
[144] *Ibid.,* 20.

This place is situated on the west side of the bay, and on our arrival it contained but few buildings. There is a large square in the center; called Portsmouth Square, on which is situated the custom house and a school-house, used for a church and a courthouse. The Parker House, a large house, fronts on the east side, and the city hotel is on the south side, on Kearny Street with Clay street between them. The ground, which as thin and sandy, rises in the rear of the town, and the land at some distance is high and uneven. No timberland is seen in every direction, nor any kind of vegetation, except a few scrubby bushes.[145]

Firewood, brought in by mules, was expensive: it cost between forty and fifty dollars a cord. Because it was so costly, it "is used only for culinary purposes."[146] Although Delavan was not a prude, he didn't like the "pernicious and detestable passion of gambling." He said,

tis here indulged to an enormous extent, and blacklegs of all colors and nations are on the alert to ease the besotted fools, of their hard-earned gold. It is not unusual for these reckless mortals to lose a handsome fortune at a sitting; and one poor idiot, an old man, was stripped of sixteen thousand dollars, all he had, in four days, at the game of monte.[147]

There were two things that surprised Delavan the most: the fact that there were piles of boxes and barrels stacked up and left for days unattended on street sides and street corners, and the extremely high prices of vacant lots.

Turning back again here to Samuel McNeil's party, they made their way on a river steamer, *South America*, to travel down the full length of the Mississippi

---

[145] *Ibid.,* 38. In 1849, the Bay's high tide often reached west to Market Street, and sometimes it even reached westward to Montgomery. Nearly all the land now known as the Tenderloin is "fill" that was brought in later.

[146] *Ibid.,* 38.

[147] *Ibid.,* 39.

River, reaching New Orleans on February 26. While attempting to cross the Gulf to Panama, their first ship sprung a leak and had to return to the Crescent City. After changing course, they took passage on another steamer, *Globe*, which took them to Brazos, Texas. There, they met an impressive looking party of soldiers "under Colonel Webb ... There, forty men from Colonel Webb's company caught cholera and died."[148] Upon leaving Brazos and Fort Brown, Texas, and crossing into northern Mexico, McNeil chafed because the majority of his party voted to buy four mules and a large wagon, which he thought was a waste of their combined assets. He also was unhappy when they made a haughty Englishman, "Mr. Perkins," leader. At the same time, in March 8, 1849,

> I selected and bought one [mule] which I rode safely and happily one thousand miles. On 8th of March, we started from Fort Brown for Reynosa (Mexico) 60 miles (west) paralleling the Rio Grande, experiencing much difficulty in keeping the road, and finding water for ourselves and mules.[149]

While Delavan reached the gold mines in mid-April, McNeil and party stopped in Durango, which author Rosen estimates had a population of "one hundred twenty five inhabitants." On April 20, 1849, McNeil noted,

> Fennifrock got sick at Durango with diarrhea. Previously he had purchased some boiled beans, fully prepared and compressed in a small space. As he was sick, he could not eat the precious mess, and gave me permission to eat some of them. I ate a small quantity, but Strode swallowed the rest at a meal.[150]

On May 10, McNeil and another member of the party almost fought a duel. At issue was McNeil's independence to strike out on his own. It was a

---

[148] Fred Rosen, *Gold: The Story of the 1848 Gold Rush and How It Shaped a Nation* (New York: Thunder's North Press, 2005), 125.

[149] *Ibid., McNeil, Travels, 126.*

[150] *Ibid.,* 140.

tense moment that might have ended in either or both men's deaths. McNeil described it in his diary.

> Before leaving, Stambaugh told me that I could do nothing without the company, and that I would certainly be murdered in California without its protection. I observed that I would rather die than travel any further with such a swindling company. This greatly enraged him, and the Lancaster lawyer picked up a gun to shoot me.[151]

McNeil carried with him a Sharpes buffalo rifle, the most powerful American rifle in existence before the Civil War. McNeil won the standoff as Stambaugh withdrew[152] his challenge. As it was, McNeil estimated that he lost one hundred dollars of personal possessions that his company of "friends" took with them. McNeil took passage by himself on the Danish schooner *Joanna Analuffa*. He paid seventy-five dollars for a ticket to sail fifteen hundred miles from Mazatlan to San Francisco. He shared the trip with two hundred other passengers, and the voyage took just over two weeks. There was a dispute with their tough German captain over the food. They were given "wormy bread, putrid jerked beef, musty rice, and miserable tea" until the passengers united to demand better food. In this case, it was the captain who had to relent. They arrived in San Francisco on May 31, 1849. It is worthwhile comparing his first impression to that of Delavan's above.

McNeil paid fifty cents to the owner of a tent to sleep on bare ground. He saw little or no evidence of any crime. "There is no law there and no need of it at present."[153] Things changed by 1850 when many more people flooded into California and the gold rush reached its peak.

While still back in Ohio, the most that McNeil had earned was about one dollar a day. But everything cost more here in California. He was also surprised by the diversity of the people he saw. "Americans, Englishmen, Hibernians.

---

[151] *Ibid.,* 143–144.
[152] Ibid., 144.
[153] *Ibid.,* 148.

Scotch folk, Chinese, Sandwich Islanders [Kanakans],[154] South Americans, New Granadians, Polanders [Poles], and Sonorians [Mexicans?]."[155] His breakfast cost $2.50. He was offered a job by the tent owner putting up muslin as a lining along walls, but he turned it down, deciding that it was time to leave for the mines the next day.

Upon reaching Sacramento in early June, McNeil was a bit thirsty.

> I entered a tent, kept by Mrs. Moore, the first American woman I had seen since leaving the States. She swore her brandy was better than any *other man's* in that renowned city. I soon found she had a great deal of the masculine gender about her and that she permitted other things [gambling?] "more expensive" in her tent than drinking brandy, considering one of her sweetest smiles worth an ounce of gold or sixteen dollars.[156]

As one of the rare members of the fairer sex, possibly she got what she asked for. Mrs. Moore charged fifty cents per glass of brandy—a high price even for the frontier. For his part, McNeil wasn't idle for long; as soon as possible, he left Sacramento to go to Smith's Bar.

In his first look at mining, he gawked at "five hundred persons" at the diggings. Smith ran a general store selling provisions and mining tools to miners. Compared to the far greater amounts greenhorns paid later for their tools, McNeil's purchases were not too expensive.

> There I paid ten dollars for a small pan for washing gold, seven dollars for a pick, and eight dollars for a small crow bar, renting a cradle for six dollars per day, I had then but seventy-five cents left.

Soon after this, he left for the North Fork of the American River, which was forty-five miles from Sacramento City. He had to pay twenty dollars to get his

---

[154] Kanakans were what the Californios and Americans called Hawaiians living in California at this time.

[155] *Ibid.,* 149.

[156] *Ibid.,* 150.

baggage moved there on mule. Already miners were building boomtowns with names like Rough and Ready, Chinese Camp, and Jackass Hill. A Georgia man had made a fortune at Rich Bar on the Middle Fork of the Feather River. On the same day McNeil arrived at Rich Bar, memories of his previous life flooded back to him.

> I slept at night on a rock, between two high mountains, with a blanket over and one under me, reflecting in wakeful time that I was 3,500 miles from home, my mind running back to my boyhood and my playmates, remembering the delicious seasons I had enjoyed with my father and mother, and particularly with my bosom friend and wife, Ellen, and my children in Lancaster, Ohio.[157]

> The next morning I commenced working in earnest and laboring incessantly for four weeks, finding, after deducting expenses, that I had cleared ten dollars per day, that is $280.00. I then sold my mining implements.[158]

McNeil returned to San Francisco, where he hoped to find letters from home waiting for him. There was only one, but he gave thanks to the steamer who'd brought it. He wrote a letter to Ellen and enclosed two hundred dollars in it along with a sample of gold dust. He then went to another location called Stanish Lou,[159] located two hundred miles south of the first place he'd worked.

> I found the miners generally making on an average, $16 per day. I saw three men dig out $9000 in seven days, and two men dig $2500 in two days. But these are rare circumstances. I saw a Spaniard having a lump of gold he had found weighing one pound and a half. Finding gold digging too hard labor for me, I returned to Sacramento city.[160]

---

[157] *Ibid.*, 152–153.
[158] *Ibid.*, 153.
[159] *Ibid.*, 153.
[160] *Ibid.*, 153.

Once he returned to Sacramento, he was fortunate to find a large sycamore tree that had stood the test of time. Its branches threw out a wide circular shade that attracted many to its coolness even before McNeil became its owner. Located halfway between the wharf and Sacramento's main street, it was the perfect spot to open a saloon. It became the city's favored watering hole. McNeil described his terms.

> I sold some brandy at my tent at twenty-five cents per drink. When a person came to me for brandy, I invariably observed if he much and would have it, and was determined to die, that I had the stuff that would kill a man as quick as any other liquor in California. This I done fully one hundred times a day.[161]

Many kinds of people frequented the Sycamore Tree Saloon. An Irishman who lived on the opposite shore of the Sacramento River was a frequent customer of McNeil's. Usually he was the classic happy drunk, but once he got into such a drunken funk that he swore he was going to kill somebody. McNeil saw him leave the bar in hot pursuit of another man. The Irishman was brandishing a Bowie knife and shouting profanities. Just as he was within a few feet of his intended victim, the man shot him with his pistol. McNeil sent word to the Irishman's wife, who rowed across the river in a rowboat. She loaded the seriously wounded man into the boat and brought him home, but he died about four hours later. There was a brief trial of the man who shot him, but he was acquitted by a miners' court. Frontier justice may seem harsh by modern standards, yet it acted as a deterrent to some kinds of crime.

McNeil described with apparent relish another case.

> A few days afterwards a man was arrested for stealing $50 worth of gold dust. A jury was called and a judge appointed, and he was found guilty, his sentence running thus: that he should have his ears cut off, receive fifty lashes on the bare back, and leave the country ... Lots were drawn to discover who should cut off his ears, and it fell upon a person named Clark.

---

[161] *Ibid.,* 158.

The prisoner prevailed upon a doctor sojourning there to do the job instead of Clark, knowing that he could do it more skillfully and will less injury; but the difference was that between a little hell and a big hell. The doctor complied with great good nature and willingness, and with a well-sharpened glittering razor, cut the scoundrel's ears off close to his head. Great good nature and willingness? [162]

After his punishment was meted out, the wretch left Sacramento city on a stolen mule. Nobody saw him again, so it isn't known whether he died of his open wounds or somehow recovered and moved on. Criminal law may have progressed in some of the states, but in the California diggings an at times haphazard kind of mob justice prevailed, at least until some years later with the institution of the federal, state, and local court system.

McNeil's account contained numerous other anecdotes, but for the sake of brevity, here is a final one. One day a doctor from Illinois entered the Sycamore Tree Establishment. He was trying to sell his horse.

"Have you been to the mines?" McNeil asked.

"I have been to the Mormon Island. I am going home, and I had only visited the region for my health. That's why I am going home."

"Any person who can endure the fatiques consequent on traveling across the Plains must have been very healthy at home."

"I would like to give (John) Fre'mont, and all the letter-writers who have extolled California, a (dose of) arsenic, as the intelligence about the gold was designed to humbug the people of the United States," the doctor replied bitterly.[163]

---

[162] *Ibid.*, 159.
[163] *Ibid.*, 161.

Many other customers at McNeil's saloon felt the same way the Illinois doctor did. He left San Francisco on or about September 2, 1849, on board the mail steamer *Panama*. McNeil was not really what one might usually think of when one thinks of a forty-niner. He didn't qualify as a true miner; he got homesick and went home. He left before he'd been in California for a full year. He did record some good stories, and when he decided it was time to leave, he sold his bar and restaurant, the Sycamore Tree Establishment, for four hundred dollars. He had accumulated another fifteen hundred dollars, mostly from his liquor and food sales at his place of business. Compared to many others, McNeil did better than most, but he didn't strike it rich.

Returning once again to James Delavan's book and his first impressions of the San Francisco Bay, on April 13, about the same time Mr. McNeil's party was still crossing northern Mexico, Mr. Delavan booked passage for twenty-five dollars on the river steamer *Placer* for Sacramento. The boat didn't get far before being grounded for three days. This gave Delavan time to observe the diversity of homelands of its many passengers.

> Our passengers were from all parts of the globe: Dutch, English, Irish, Scots, French, Peruvians, Mexicans, Chilians, Sandwich Islanders, Oregonians; some from the Atlantic States, and even from New South Wales.[164]

The boat was so completely packed with passengers and their baggage that Delavan compared their sleeping arrangement to sardines in a can. As soon as he arrived in Sacramento, he recorded the scene.

> While at Sacramento, I had an opportunity of seeing all sorts of people, from the wild Indian to the more wild-looking Oregonians, with hair untrimmed and *unkempt* their faces covered with abundant growth of beard, rough and razor-able, and innocent of soap, if one might judge from appearances ... These rude woodsmen, clad in buckskin garments, soiled and greasy, mounted on horseback upon saddles high before and

---

[164] *Ibid.,* 41.

behind, and equipped with spurs peculiar to California and Mexico, large and heavy, would dash the place at full speed.[165]

While in Sacramento, Delavan noticed that prices of everything there were even greater than they were in San Francisco. He also noted, "And then enormous prices continued to increase as you approach the mines."[166] This trend toward inflated prices the nearer one got to the actual mining regions became an omnipresent reality all miners had to face throughout the early gold rush years of this study, from 1848 through 1851.

Almost from the first second he arrived at Coloma, Delavan started to work. He stated he was satisfied to be bringing in an ounce of gold per day. It seemed to him that

> Colloma [Residents later dropped one of the "l"s in their town's name] began to assume the appearance of a town. Several families from Oregon were there. Individuals of the softer sex were rare, and the specimens were unattractive; still civilization seemed advancing ... Newcomers were constantly arriving, some having crossed the country through Mexico, and some by the isthmus, and others from the Lord knows where.[167]

Delavan traveled to nearby diggings, including South Fork and Weaver's Creek. He was impressed to learn of another strike of Kelsey's, between Weaver's Creek and the South Fork, some seven miles southeast of Coloma. He made two trips to Big Bar. On his second visit, while on his way from Coloma to Big Bar, he confronted a large rattler that had fourteen rattles. This number of rattles indicated it was fourteen years old. Using his pistol, Delavan shot it.

> To my great joy, I discovered the *serpent* writhing in his agony, and with his head nearly severed from his trunk. I gazed upon the varying hues of his chequered skin of black and green, and

---

[165] *Ibid.*, 47.

[166] *Ibid.*, 50.

[167] *Ibid.*, 61.

blessed my stars that I had not felt the deadly fang to which I had been nearly exposed.[168]

It is worth pausing a moment here to appreciate how relieved Delavan felt to have just been able to take his next breath. He moved on to Volcano Bar, where he observed some men using a diving bell to excavate a river bed. When he arrived at Big Bar, Delavan noticed that a great deal of work had been done since his earlier visit.

> A bracket-dam at the head of the Bar, by which a small part had been drained; and this had been worked to enormous profit, yielding three or four ounces a day to each of pure gold in coarse grains. Such was the success of an association of limited means, and operating against many disadvantages.[169]

A few days later, Delavan left Big Bar on August 26 to head back to San Francisco by way of Coloma. He had sent some important items around the Horn on the *Brooklyn*, which he needed to claim.

He traveled with a friend. When the two men arrived at Coloma, they were nearly exhausted, grimy, and starved. Fortunately, they

> were glad to find the progress of civilization such, that for a California price (12 s. [shillings] a meal) we could have supper and room upon the floor for the night.[170]

Delavan was impressed by the amount of new construction at Coloma on both sides of the river. As happened to many who thought they were buying a ticket for a fairly comfortable stage ride, when he purchased a ticket at the Coloma stage office to ride the fifty miles to Sacramento, it turned out that he went in a wooden, horse-drawn wagon without shock absorbers, which gave him and two Irishmen a rough ride. After a brief stay in Sacramento, he took a

---

[168] *Ibid.*, 100.

[169] *Ibid.*, 102.

[170] *Ibid.*, 104.

steamer to San Francisco, arriving there in early September. Like many others, he was shocked to find high prices.

The poor congregated in a slum called Happy Valley. Potable water was scarce. Delavan found that water sold for three cents per bucket. On the newly built California Street,

> a house, imported from Liverpool, by English merchants, who were here at the first discovery of gold. The frame of this structure was cast iron, with doors, window frames, and shutters of iron, and the covering of which was zinc ... Vessels at anchor in the bay, were used; and the storage, which for a bulk equivalent to that of a barrel of flour, was at the rate of three dollars a month, produced enormous revenues.[171]

Clearly, California and Great Britain were already linked in many ways through commerce, banking, finance, and gold and silver mining.

By way of Stockton, Delavan toured for some distance along the San Joaquin River Valley. He praised the branches of it, and especially the Stanislaus River, as being the region where some of the richest claims had been found.

In late October 1849, Delavan returned for the last time to San Francisco. He was impressed by three newer ships that were in service.

> I found facilities of ascending the Sacramento greatly increased. A small steamer, built in the Bay, called the *Mint*, was making regular trips, as was the propeller, *M'Kim*, first came round Cape Horns from New Orleans, and was purchased by Simmons & Hutchinson. But the best vessel was the *Senator* which was long given up for lost, but afterwards arrived from the Atlantic, after a passage of seven months.[172]

---

[171] *Ibid.*, 121–122. Delavan sailed from San Francisco before the city was almost completely destroyed by the Christmas Eve 1849 fire. The English merchants who brought the cast-iron house from Liverpool may have had a premonition that fires would become the greatest danger to early San Francisco. For more info on these fires, see Robert Graysmith, *Black Fire* (New York: Crown Publishers, 2012).

[172] *Ibid.*, 127.

For $150, Delavan bought passage on a slow steamer, the *California*. Although it was advertised to sail November 1 for Panama, the captain had to delay weighing anchor until dawn of the following day. The delay was caused by the arrival of another vessel, *Panama*, which, years before this, had brought such famous immigrants as William Gwin and David C. Broderick to San Francisco. The *Panama* carried mail that had priority over everything else at the time in San Francisco.

Delavan was happy to sleep on the deck of the slow-moving *California*. At this time, Delavan, like most of the passengers, fretted that the captain decided to conserve fuel rather than keeping the coal-burning boilers going full blast. It was November 22 when the steamer finally anchored in Panama Bay.

This time, Delavan made his way from west to east across the tropical isthmus of Panama. Going part of the way by small boat, he was ultimately cheered.

> As we approached the coast, our ears were pleasingly saluted by the roaring of the surf, as it washed the shores of the bay; and soon our eyes were gratified by the sight of lights of Chagres … and, none, unless similarly situated, can realize our satisfaction when we were alongside the *Falcon*, and prepared to mount her decks.[173]

The contrast between this trip on the *Falcon* and his original one going west almost couldn't have been greater. This time, perhaps in part because the captain knew Delavan, he had a good stateroom and excellent service on their voyage across the Gulf of Mexico to Cuba. He changed to a much larger ship, the *Ohio*, in Havana on December 3. Except for bad weather around Cape Hatteras, Delavan's final voyage to New York went uneventfully. He docked in New York on December 9.

On the final page of his account, Delavan commented on choosing the best route to California from the East Coast. He was sure that the second choice, to sail to Chagres on the east coast of Panama and to cross the isthmus, was the best route out of the five options. In conclusion he added, "For, by 'such tribulations' only, can any aspirant for adventure reach the 'Golden Gates' of California."[174]

---

[173] *Ibid.*, 151.
[174] *Ibid.*, 155.

CHAPTER 6
Israel and Titus Hale

We heard by the Parkers that the team that was two and three weeks behind us at the Willow Springs and the Black Hills had no grass at all and that the men, women and children were seen sitting by the roadside (sadly) [Parentheses, Mr. Hale's] weeping and lamenting the situation of themselves and teams. Also we had a report from ahead that the grass was poor for sixty miles.[175]

—Israel Hale's diary, August 8, 1849

It is reported that the men who lost their oxen tracked them up and found all but one; they in possession of ten or twelve Indians, and the men killed seven Indians and took five horses from them. The company were ["was"] from Jefferson City, Missouri. I give the above as I heard it, but do not vouch for the truth of it ... We are perfectly covered with dust and everything about us is in the same situation. How our cattle stand it I am unable to say, for it is often the case that we cannot see oxen or wagon for the dust, consequently have to drive at random.[176]

—Israel Hale's diary, August 11, 1849, as his wagon train entered the most arid region of western Nevada

During the spring of 1849, Israel Hale, a native of Glastonbury, Connecticut, who later became a middle-aged Missouri resident, came down with a serious case of gold fever. Israel and his wife talked it over and decided on

---

[175] *Ibid.,* 107–108.
[176] *Ibid.,* 106–107.

taking the risk: they would bet the ranch that Israel and his seventeen-year-old son, Titus, could net more by placer mining gold in California than by continuing to work the farm in Missouri. The forty-five-year-old Israel left his family, his wife, and several younger children for what he knew full well might be a waste of time and money. With having to endure unendurable hardships, plus the real possibly of being killed, Israel and Titus had to cross two thousand miles of prairie, climb high mountains, and trudge through rugged California country, facing death from diseases, accidents, and Indian attacks just to reach this promised land of gold. What their lives had been like before this is something of a mystery. Israel's account ended with their arrival in Sacramento. He added to this diary at the end of each day on the trail, often under bad circumstances of bitterly cold weather. Summarizing briefly in his final comments, Israel stated he would have written more except for being too sick many times. After all, he was doing it as "a present from one who feels a greater interest in their welfare than any other person living," meaning his youngest children.[177] To introduce his background, Israel's mother, Sarah Hale, had died giving birth to Israel in Connecticut in 1804. Little is known about his father or grandparents.

In early May 1849, Israel and Titus packed a wagon, selected a number of their hardier looking cattle, hitched the wagon to a team of oxen, and rode away from their home in Manchester, Missouri, heading southwest for St. Joseph, the rendezvous point for many Great Plains emigrant gold seekers.

> At twelve o'clock we left St. Joseph for Savannah Landing. The rain on the previous night made the road (which is very hilly) quite slippery and bad until we arrived at the Missouri [River] bottom where we had to encounter deep mud for two or three miles.[178]

After much "pulling," at eleven o'clock on the morning of May 6, they arrived at the landing. Right away, they realized they certainly weren't alone;

---

[177] Israel Foote Hale, "Diary of Trip to California in 1849," *Quarterly of the Society of California Pioneers,* ed. Henry L. Byrne, (San Francisco: Society of California Pioneers Board of Directors, 1925), 130.

[178] *Ibid.,* 61.

there were many other emigrant parties already there, each one awaiting its turn to cross.

> Found at the landing about thirty wagons ahead of us waiting to cross. Spent the balance of the day in cooking, cleaning up, etc. Got the privilege of using the boats at night by manning them and paying an extra price for crossing. Mine was the thirteenth wagon and was crossed about sun rise Monday morning [May 7, 1849].[179]

Unlike James Delavan and Samuel McNeil, Israel Hale didn't make the journey to California in order to write a how-to book, later to be published and sold to the public. Hale's account wasn't published during the nineteenth century. He was a perceptive emigrant who kept his eyes open and his mind clear of many of the prevailing prejudices about race, culture, and religion held by many, even most of his contemporaries. Late in the afternoon of May 9, they began moving, crossing many steep hills for "eight miles" until they hit Wolf River.

> The country is becoming more level but is still some hilly. Saw the first Indian this day. Since we crossed the Missouri we find plenty of good spring water at almost every camp. On Wolf River we saw an Indian grave yard near the river. After crossing Wolf River we saw some land for farming purposes. Last night we stood guard for the first time. This afternoon we saw several Indians. It is said that a large encampment is very near.[180]

In his next entry, Israel noted the death and burial of Nathaniel Clark from cholera. His train moved westward to the Blue River. He compared it to "the Maramec but not so wide.[181] There, they saw provisions left by a previous train, dumped and discarded to lighten its load.

---

[179] *Ibid.*, 61.
[180] *Ibid.*, 61.
[181] *Ibid.*, 62.

The next day, they marched more than twenty miles. As was the case a couple of nights before, it was cool. There seemed to be a threat of rain.

> This day we passed some fine country but very little timber or water. We passed several graves during the day and the road is nearly filled with wagons and teams; as many as eight or ten trains in sight at one time, and some of them large.[182]

Mr. Hale and his son certainly were not the only gold fever patients. The next few days of travel were uneventful except for the sighting of two Pawnee Indians at some distance away. The nights had become colder. They were bothered in the evenings by June bugs that were brown and red in color. They weren't in any danger of becoming lost because they were among so many others.

> Most of the teams are now making a rush for the South Pass, distance thirty-six miles. Two hundred and fifty teams are within eight or ten miles behind and near five hundred between here and Fort Laramie. It is said there are about eight or ten hundred ahead of us.[183]

Suddenly, it dawned on his team that they were involved in the gold rush, where every man was trying to get to the California mines before others could. On July 1, they were in sight of snow-covered mountains of the Rockies, including Sweetwater Mountain. Because their oxen bordered on exhaustion, they knocked off earlier than planned. Meanwhile, they were bothered by dust and again by the cold. On July 6, they paid six dollars for a ferry to cross the Green River. Israel thought it looked like the Maramec, the same river mentioned above and one he was familiar with in Missouri. His entry for July 9 read,

> Between three and five o'clock we crossed the river [Green River] and about the same time swam the cattle over. We found on the west side several half-breed Indians-traders. They bought

---

[182] *Ibid.,* 62.
[183] *Ibid.,* 87.

and sold at their own price. Alkali is still abundant and we see more or less stock lying dead every day, some from the effect of poisoned water, others hard driving.[184]

They passed Ham's Fork, or Fontinell's Fork, on Green River. Then,

We passed a place where they were bringing a man by the name of Merill [Merrill?], of Lexington, Missouri, that was killed by a wagon. We also passed a train of U.S. Troops going to Bear River to build a fort.[185]

Hale noted that about a fourth of the men in their train were sick. Whether it was due to disease or simply because of becoming too weary to go on, many had decided to quit. "In starting we had more than twenty wagons. It is now reduced to eight."[186]

When they reached the Bear River, they found abundant grass and water. Hale reported the river was not as wide as the Maramec but deeper. Overnight water in a pan froze so hard "that it could be turned over without losing its contents."[187] At least up until this point, any contacts they had had with Indians were mutually peaceful. They crossed the Bear River on July 14. "We encamped near some Indians. They have commenced visiting our camp."[188] On the next day, July 15, he wrote,

For the first time since we left St. Joseph we rested on Sunday, or rather rested our teams. The cause of it was that one of the men that belonged to Tindell's wagon was very sick and he could not stand travel. Soon after breakfast was over Mr. Smith, a mountaineer, came to our camp. Soon after several other persons called in and if I am not mistaken, they had a jolly day of it. As for myself it was wash day with me. Several gangs of

---

[184] *Ibid.,* 89.

[185] *Ibid.,* 89.

[186] *Ibid.,* July 9, 1849.

[187] *Ibid.,* July 12, 1849.

[188] *Ibid.,* 91.

Indians called during the day, the more especially about meal
time. These Indians appear to be well off and have large gangs
of horses. Our sick man is no better this evening.[189]

Stress, fatigue, and depression took a toll. The train had to "lay by"
another day. Game had become scarce, but they had been getting by, killing
"some mountain sheep, antelope, and some black tail deer. Occasionally they
kill a white bear."[190] There were no more buffalo. By May 24, "Three miles
from Fort Neuf we came to the Pannack River." He noted it was "one hundred
twenty yards wide and four or five inches deep." They also had to get through
a slough before coming out in a "valley of the Snake or Lewis Rivers."[191]
They were plagued by "a quantity of dust." They lost time whenever they
didn't post a guard over their cattle at night; they had to spend the morning
searching the desert for their lost cattle. Their journey westward was a
continuous learning experience. Emigrants didn't have garages. On July 27,
his entry read,

> The creek on which we encamped last night is thought by some
> to be Raft River. The road ran up this creek and we followed
> until noon. There appeared to be a road that ran toward Lewis
> River that we supposed to be the Oregon Road. Passed two
> graves today, a man and a woman, one buried in '46, the other
> in '47. I exchanged the four wheels of the wagon this morning ...
> Heavy wind last few days; much dust.[192]

It was some comfort to know they were on a trail others on their way to
California or Oregon had passed over before. Those who successfully crossed
the continent had to be strong, experienced, and resilient enough to make
necessary repairs along the way. They were encouraged by other whites, like
the "mountaineer Smith" described above, who said their train had arrived

---

[189] *Ibid.,* 91–92.

[190] *Ibid.,* 92.

[191] *Ibid.,* 95.

[192] *Ibid.,* 97.

at the foot of the Rockies earlier in the year than many in previous years. On Sunday, July 28, they could see much snow and frost. It was "very cold at night."

> Last night, after we encamped, another of my oxen died. He was in fine order this morning ... In the afternoon we followed the valley about two miles where the road took through a gap in the mountain. It was narrow but wide enough for a road. We went round one peak and found that the road from the Salt Lake entered about this time.[193]

Livestock, albeit oxen, cattle, horses, or mules, were good companions as well as being their sole means of transportation, whether they were emigrants who arrived in California by ship or overland. On the California Trail, cattle were especially useful for milk and butter. If food was short, any livestock could be slaughtered for meat. On Sunday, July 29, they passed Steeple Rock "from ten to fifty feet in height."[194] They had been on the trail for three complete months, but two more months lay ahead of them before reaching Sacramento.

At sunup August 1, eleven of their cattle were missing. They found nine before they happened upon a man who had the other two. He told them he thought they belonged to a train that was ahead of them. On the next day, they bypassed

> some bad water but did not stop long. We then drove near eight miles further and stopped for the night with good grass, no wood but water for stock for use by digging. We were endebted [indebted] to Mr. John Hutson for digging a well, which we gave the name Hutson's Well.[195]

Soon after they came to a fork of the road, one member of their train, John Sutton, took the left fork and wasn't back to camp at nightfall. The next day, Sunday, some went after him while others hunted or fished. The hunters

---

[193] *Ibid., 98.*

[194] *Ibid., 98.*

[195] *Ibid., 100.*

returned with "some hares and birds." It was the fishermen who had the most luck, bringing in "five mountain trout." The same evening, there was a rare sprinkle of rain. The next day, Sutton returned, and Hale noticed a snow-covered mountain,

> which is something I did not expect to see until we arrived at the Sierra Nevada. We had fine grass, good water and willow wood. As we were coming through the canyon I saw one wagon turned over and a cart that had been broken down. The cart was abandoned, the wagon was broken but was being repaired.[196]

At about this time, there was talk about many horses being stolen from the trains. Some suggested that Indians had stolen them. Israel withheld judgment while noting their value,

> One was taken but a short distance from our camp. It is laid to the Indians and probably is, but I think some white men may be at the head of it. Horses are very valuable here. A good horse in order would bring one hundred and fifty dollars and a pony that could be bought in the States for twenty-five would here bring seventy five or one hundred dollars.[197]

Here he noted the land around them would be good for farming.

> It is not as large as Big River in Jefferson County, Missouri, but it appears to be increasing in size as we follow it down.

> Another wagon left our train yesterday [August 7]. It was Jamison that formerly lived on Mrs. Rennock's Place. We have but six wagons left in the train.[198]

---

196 *Ibid.,* 101.
197 *Ibid.,* 101.
198 *Ibid.,* 103.

If conditions had been hard before this, things now began getting even harder. What happened to Jamison is not clear from Hale's account. Perhaps Jamison was in such a hurry to reach the gold fields in the California territory that he simply struck out on his own and perished. Perhaps he joined a train ahead of Hale's. For numerous reasons, he left. It was clear that the Hales' team was in greater peril than ever.

During the evening of August 7, they passed by the carcass of an ox Indians had killed. Hale thought that the meat would still be good even though it hadn't been salted. He added that in his own experience, he'd eaten meat that was "eight or ten days old."

On Sunday, August 12, he noticed how the temperature went from very cold to hot in the space of a few hours. He wore his overcoat until ten in the morning. After crossing a river,

> Mr. Jeffries of Union [Missouri?] came to our company today. Cattle are stolen almost every day. Night before last [August 10–11] almost twenty were taken. Last night the rise of that number were taken.[199]

On August 13, they drove forward ten miles, stopping around noon, where the grass was poor. Losses of livestock were so serious that Indians were about to be shot and killed. Hale remarked,

> It is reported that the men who lost their oxen tracked them up and found all but one; they in possession of ten or twelve Indians, and the men killed seven Indians and took five horses from them. The company were [was] from Jefferson City, Missouri. I give the above as I heard it, but do not vouch for the truth of it ... We are perfectly covered with dust and everything about us is in the same situation. How our cattle stand it I am unable to say, for it is often the case that we cannot see oxen or wagon for the dust, consequently have to drive at random.[200]

---

[199] *Ibid.*, 106.
[200] *Ibid.*, 106–107.

Although the conditions they were forced to endure were terribly difficult, there were other parties they got word of who suffered even more. On August 14, he noted,

> We heard by the Parkers that the team that was two and three weeks behind us at the Willow Springs and the Black Hills had no grass at all and that the men, women and children were seen sitting by the roadside (sadly) weeping and lamenting the situation of themselves and teams. Also we had a report from ahead that the grass was poor for sixty miles.[201]

The report went on with more dire news. Supposedly, they were going to have to travel "one hundred and sixty miles" further before reaching the Sink of the Humboldt River, the stream they were following. In addition, "there were six hundred herd of dead cattle between here and the Sink."[202]

Despite now having fewer wagons in his train, the Hales were never lacking in news from other trains about losses of livestock and violent clashes with Indians. On August 15, Hale's train left the valley they'd been in for the past couple of days and drove some ten miles farther on the Humboldt River before encamping.

> Our grass is not good but the cattle are feeding on willow leaves and some coarse grass.

> Five or ten cattle were stolen last night from our camp. I saw a man from a train camped two or three miles below us that told me they did not guard their stock last night; that their company was large and their young men wanted sport and concluded to let the Indians steal them an opportunity to go after them and shoot the Indians, and I have no doubt that they could make a raise of horses from the Indians, as several others had done

---

[201] *Ibid.*, 107–108.
[202] *Ibid.*, 108.

who had lost oxen, but the Indians were too smart. They did not touch them.[203]

In the same entry, Israel observed,

> These Diggers are a small Indian or rather short and have very few guns but are armed with bows and arrows. They are seldom seen or near the road, but they keep themselves concealed during the day, and in the night leave their ambush and sally forth in search of plunder. It has been their custom to cripple stock in such a way that it would become useless to the owner and they would leave it, when the Indians would return and carry off the meat.[204]

Mr. Hale stated in the same entry that this year, the Indians had changed their tactics to where they now were simply driving off the livestock. His train had observed several abandoned wagons on the road. The emigrants had had to abandon their journeys and either turn back or possibly find other wagon trains they could join. Two days later on the trail, he noted one wagon burned and another abandoned.

At this point, they usually logged from five to twenty miles per day. During the next two days, they had an intermittent, slight sprinkle of rain. Israel commented that it was not even as much as "Missouri dew." Already they had come a long way, but the hardest part of their journey still lay ahead. By August 19,

> We suppose that we are between eighty or one hundred miles from the Sink.

> We still find wagons, or parts of wagons and dead cattle by the road side and at old camping places, but we find no provisions thrown away about here. We have a great many that call to stay

---

[203] *Ibid.,* 108.

[204] *Ibid.,* 108.

all night, generally foot men. Some say their teams have given out and some are lost from their trains, others have left their trains; some propose paying, but they are mostly begging order and endeavor to pay by telling some great tale respecting the route. We at first entertained these travelers, but we learned that many imposters were on the road and at the present time it takes a very smooth and straight talk to get accommodations in our train.[205]

The number of wagons in their party rose to eleven, including the Hales'. On August 16, Israel reported, "The Franklin County Company came into our out train today." He added in an upbeat note,

> Messrs. Berry, Hensly, Sutton and Boley join our mess in hunting and fishing, and with the game we have pot pies, soups, stews, fish frys etc. Some of our dishes would be called fine even in the States ... the road has been good most of the day.[206]

As the party to which the Hale's team belonged grew a little, Indian thefts were on the rise.

> Every day I hear of depredations being committed by the Indians. They stole a lot of cattle from a company called Helltown Greasers and I have not heard of they getting them. They stole a lot from one company and they pursued them and found that the cattle had been driven through a narrow pass in the mountain and finally came in sight of them, but in possession of Indians. They had them so fixed in the mountain that they could roll stones down and prevent any person from ascending and there they were, shaking their blankets, halloeing and bidding defiance to the whites, who had lost the cattle, although the cattle were in plain sight.[207]

[205] *Ibid.* 111.

[206] *Ibid.,* 109.

[207] *Ibid.,* 109.

On August 16, Israel noted,

> I understand that forty or fifty men are now engaged in the
> matter but how it will terminate I cannot say, as the Indians
> are beyond rifle shot and cannot be approached by the white
> men for fear of the rolling rocks from above, which they are
> well supplied with. And the mountain is three quarters of a
> mile wide high and can only be ascended in one place, owing
> to the steepness of it. The termination I am told I will endeavor
> to note if I hear how it results.... I am told that the Helltown
> Greasers have got back a portion of their cattle but did not have
> the particulars.[208]

Hale did not note how the confrontation between the party of whites and
the Indians on the mountain ended because his next entry was four days later,
on August 20. It was also from along the Humboldt River road in Nevada.

> The Humboldt is a long river for one of its size. It varies but little
> in size from Big River. We have been on its waters sixteen days
> and have no knowledge when we shall leave it, for we cannot
> learn the distance to the Sink. The water is getting bad and the
> grass nearly given out. Willows will soon be all that our cattle
> can get.[209]

Another incident involving Indians, stolen cattle, and angry white
emigrants came a few days later.

> Some few days since, a train lost some cattle and thirty men
> started in pursuit. They divided into companies, most of seven
> each. One company, however, had but four men in it. This
> company came across four Indians, and walked up towards
> them intending to take them prisoners, but when they got

---

[208] *Ibid.,* 109–110.
[209] *Ibid.,* August 20, 1849.

within bow shot of the Indians they shot their arrows at them and wounded three of the white men: one in the shoulder, one in the forehead, the other in the wrist. The white men killed three Indians and one ran away. I understand that one Indian wounded all three of the men and had two wounds himself and when he found that the white men would catch him, as he had shot all his arrows, he stopped and told the man to shoot him in the head, which he did. The company found their cattle but they had all been killed.[210]

The Indians who stole the cattle were the same ones the white vigilantes found and confronted. This makes the way Israel reported it seem more reliable as being truly factual.

In his next entry, Hale noted being told by Mr. Green, who was from Franklin County and had passed the same way, that they might find a mountain with "a lower gap" in it if they didn't take the road to the Sink. Israel added, "Furthermore that we could get to the Sacramento in nine days travel and mentioned the route of Myers and Hudspeth as shorter."[211] Their route might have been easier if they had continued toward the Sink, but Hale's train took the cutoff. On August 22, Hale wrote,

This morning we took the cutoff, if it is one. It takes off at a point where the Humboldt runs south and the cut-off runs a west course to a gap in the mountain. It starts in a valley and several miles from the road is seen a round mound. [It] appears to be in or near the center of the valley. We drove through sage about eight or nine miles and then took into the gap or pass in the mountain.[212]

As they approached three springs of water, they had to hold back their

---

[210] *Ibid.,* 113. Although it is improbable that Edward Prime happened upon the remains of the same Indian's body who was shot in the head, it is just barely possible.

[211] *Ibid.,* 113

[212] *Ibid.,* 114.

cattle from drinking because there were three other teams ahead of them. Hale's party pushed on again to some other wells, where his cattle were able to quench their thirst.

After passing Rabbit Hole Springs, his team came to a grisly sight. It was August 22.

> We have passed a great many dead cattle and as many that were not dead but had given out and had been left to die. We have not seen fifty spears of grass since we left this road and had but one chance for water and that in a small quantity and of indifferent quality.[213]

On the following day, a man "from the Black Rock Springs" said they had to "hurry and get through the Salt Plain before the heat of the day." While they tried to speed up, they were slowed.

> Our cattle were then nearly worn down, having traveled between thirty and forty miles without food and but one sip of water. But go ahead we must and as fast as possible. We reached the Salt Plain about eleven o'clock and a very warm morning. We thought of stopping until the cool of the evening before we took the plain but our cattle had been without food for thirty hours and that would not do.[214]

As August 23 wore on,

> About this time clouds began to appear and shield us from the heat and shocking rays of the sun. The wind began to blow and in a short time it was thick and cloudy and we had a strong wind from the south which took the whole of the dust from drive and oxen. We had a slight sprinkle of rain and we drove on and just got through the plain as the wind fell and the sun again made

---

[213] *Ibid.,* 114.
[214] *Ibid.,* 114–115.

its appearance. It was certainly a great blessing sent upon us by the Hand of the Almighty, for if it had continued on as warm we would not have come through the plain without losing more or less of our stock, but as it was we came through safe and without the loss of a single steer. This plain is from six to eight miles wide. It is covered with a whitish crust and entirely void of vegetation of any kind.[215]

After this close call, they drove about five miles. Then,

We found a large number of wagons encamped among others a train of United States Troops. They are on their way from Oregon to meet troops from the States and assist them if necessary on their way to California. If they do not need their assistance they will render such assistance to emigrants as they may need.[216]

On the following day, August 26, they were reminded of another deadly incident between whites and Indians, indicating that they were no longer in a relatively safe region like they'd once been back east or anywhere in the States.

Yesterday they sent four men to search for a road from here to Humboldt; thinking that a better and more direct route could be had and more grass and water, but on the route two of the men went up on the mountain to take observations. While there they saw two Indians coming. They professed to be Snakes, but as soon as they came near enough they shot one of the men dead and wounded the other. The man that was wounded killed one of Indians and the other fled. The other men were at the foot of the mountain with the horses. The wounded man gave the alarm and the three men brought in the corpse which is to be interred today.[217]

---

215 *Ibid.,* 115.
216 *Ibid.,* 118.
217 *Ibid.,* 118.

Sometimes Israel used the term *mountain* even when he meant a range of mountains, like either the Rockies or the Sierra Nevada. The constant pressures of hard bumps and long drives on the trail began to take a heavy toll on their equipment and wagons.

> The Salt Valley is nearly surrounded with mountains. And is of an irregular shape ... There is scarcely a wagon wheel in our train that has a tight tire upon it. Then pegs in shoes and boots come loose and the hoe nearly falls to pieces. This has been the case for hundreds of miles back, but I think not to such an extent as at this place.[218]

Mr. Hale's diary contained many observations of unusual features in the terrain. He also carefully noted features of timber forests and prairie that he thought were unusual or of land suited for farming. Here, however, they were still not finished looking at desert.

> Ten miles from Salt Valley, we came to High Rock Canyon. I saw very high pillars ... I saw a round hill on our left that reminded me of Chimney Rock. I passed one place that reminded me of Pine Street in New York-the rocks were perpendicular on both sides. The canyon seems to have been formed by nature for a road.[219]

When cattle and horses became sick, the emigrants did what they could to help them survive. For some readers today, their treatments might seem to be primitive, even harmful.

> I find that the long dry stretch has injured our teams very much. They all appear weak, dull and sluggish and I am fearful

---

[218] *Ibid.,* 118.

[219] *Ibid.,* 119. At the bottom of this page is an unlabeled footnote: "These rocks, by a writer for the *New York Herald,* are said to be seven hundred feet high. He may have measured them, but I had no time. I thought I would put it low enough."

that we may lose some of them yet. Some the hollow horn; for that we bore the horn and put in salt, pepper, and water until it run out of their noses. They have another disease called the hollow tail; for that they split the tail where it is hollow. Two teams left this morning in consequence of the steers being weak and sick; and about ten o'clock another team left for the same cause. The last team has come up, having given the team a little rest, and also let them feed awhile.[220]

Bonds were formed between individual emigrants on the long and stressful journey that lasted lifetimes. They had to cooperate in order to survive. At night, the temperature became so cold that once again water froze hard in pans when turned upside down at dawn. They wore their overcoats in the mornings until ten o'clock, and sometimes later, to keep warm.

On September 3, their party reached the highest point of the Sierras on the Lawson Trail. Israel's entry reflected an unusual accident where others were lucky they weren't killed or injured.

While I was on the rocky summit or point, I had a fine view of the road and had counted, I think, twenty-eight teams and as my eye reached the Summit I saw a heavy laden wagon driven by ten yoke of oxen start rapidly down the mountain. The chain attached to the wagon had broken just as they had reached the Summit. It was two or three hundred feet, taking the wheel steers with it and luckily turned bottom upward. Many saw it and as many rejoiced to see it turn over, for had it continued to follow the road it must have destroyed considerable property, if not some lives. As it was, the chain and an ox yoke was about the amount.[221]

The next day, they drove about ten miles. As they approached California for the first time, he was struck by the novelty of traveling through thick

---

[220] *Ibid.*, 121.
[221] *Ibid.*, 125.

timber. He noted that most of the trees were pine, although some were firs. He concluded with this entry: "We had a steep hill to come up and after an hour or so a similar one to go down, when we came down to Goose Lake."[222] On September 11, after driving through rough country, they found some water. Here he noted, "The Indians are bad. They shot one ox last night eleven times and I am told that four or five more were shot in another company."[223]

As a number of emigrants fell ill, they were plagued by rumors about how far they possibly still had to go. On September 12, Hale reported,

> It appears we are to lay by another day. Robert Harper is sick and several others in the train and a black boy died last night in Campbell's train; also they have some sick and our cattle need rest very much ... At one time we hear the distance to the mines is not more than twenty miles and perhaps in an hour we will hear it is between two and three hundred.[224]

Tensions between individuals rose over the scarce food they had to eat.

> Provisions are becoming a little scarce at this time [September 12]. Flour and bacon will bring twenty-five cents per pound each; beef twelve and one half, sugar and coffee from fifty to seventy-five cents, but those that have will not part with in unless to a friend and then it is loaned to be returned in California. In consequence of living on salt meat without vegetable so great a length of time, many of the emigrants are troubled with the scurvy. Bowel complaint and fevers are also very common, neither does the sickness appear to decrease, but rather increase.[225]

Israel's and the team's troubles continued even as they were surprised by a

---

[222] *Ibid.,* 125–126.

[223] *Ibid.,* 128.

[224] *Ibid.,* 128.

[225] *Ibid.,* 129.

party of visitors headed east. This occurred as they approached John Lawson's famous rancho.

> Last evening the United States Engineer arrived from the settlements with his attendants and gave us a way bill. The distance Is one hundred and forty miles and a large portion of the road is bad, it being over mountains. They had among them several invalids and I sold them one ounce of quinine for twenty dollars. We lay by for another day for the benefit of the sick and the teams.[226]

The engineer was on a mission looking for a suitable route across the mountains for a future railroad.[227] He needed help and attempted to hire some men from Campbell's team. Israel gleaned whatever information he could from them,

> These men speak of money being very plentiful, but say the health of the country is bad. Had to wait after the 15th six more days for Bassett and Hemstead had the flux.[228]

It was depressing to be so close to their destination, but with many who had fallen ill. They had to pass through steep mountains as well as hills "from five to twenty miles per day." On September 15, Hale noted,

> We also passed some of the finest pine forests I have ever seen. The road for the most of the way was through pine except the valleys, which are prairies and generally a fine stream of clear, cold water running through them.[229]

---

[226] *Ibid.*, 129.

[227] Already in 1849, many political leaders, including John B. Weller (the fifth California governor) and future president Abraham Lincoln, were planning the prospective route of a transcontinental US railroad. See Frank H. Baumgardner III, *Killing for Land in Early California* (New York: Algora Publishing, 2005).

[228] *Ibid.*, 129.

[229] *Ibid.*, 129.

In one of his final entries, Hale related that water was scarce. He explained why they had trouble that delayed their arrival.

> Many teams gave out and many wagons were left; but we at last reached the settlement in the Sacramento Valley. We then had one hundred and fifteen miles to travel before we reached the city. We arrived on the fifteenth of October, but were forced to lay by with the sick; that made us so late getting in.[230]

Israel's last words described what he actually saw in Sacramento.

> The city is below the mouth of the American Fork on the Sacramento River. It has been lately built and is quite large, but most of the buildings are covered with cloth. A large business is doing, but the largest dealers are those that keep provisions. There is lying at the landing about twenty vessels of all classes, from a good sized ship to the smallest class of sloop. The valley is said to be from forty to one hundred miles. It contains much fine land but a portion is at time inundated.

> Timber is found on the banks of the river in abundance. It is the live oak. Back from the river we find nothing but prairies. Another city is now laid out above the American Fork. It is called New Boston. I am now encamped six miles above the city [Sacramento?] on the Sacramento for the purpose of resting ourselves and cattle before starting for the mines and have been since the fifteenth, it now being the twenty-second of the month.[231]

In his final paragraph, Israel said that he might have written more except for the fact that he had been ill part of the time, and too often the circumstances were unfavorable for writing. In his final, slightly cryptic remark, he meant

---

[230] *Ibid.*, 130.
[231] *Ibid.*, 130.

his diary to be "a present from one who feels a greater interest in their welfare than any other person living."[232]

Israel Hale and his son Titus went on to become successful miners. About two years after he arrived in California, Israel returned home to his family with what the Society of California Pioneers' quarterly journal editor, Henry C. Byrne, wrote in the foreword as, "something more than $1,500 in California gold dust."[233]

---

[232] Ibid., 132.

[233] *Ibid.,* foreword. Israel's "something over $1,500 in gold dust" would be worth $125,414.68 in today's dollars. Not bad for working for just over a year in the mines.

Courtesy of Bancroft Library, University of California, Berkeley, California

CHAPTER 7

Nelson Kingsley:
A Homesick Argonaut

Captain Bottom: "Ahoy! Where are you from?"

English captain: "From England and Lisbon."

Captain Bottom: "Where are you bound?"

English captain: "To Tampico."

Captain Bottom: "Do you want anything?"

English captain: "No."

Captain Bottom: "Will you allow us to come on board and send letters?"

English captain: "Yes."

—Brief dialogue at sea between two ship captains in the mid-Atlantic, April 13, 1849

Nelson Kingsley sailed for California gold country in the spring of 1849.[2] He was a gifted musician, choir singer, and poet whose trade was carpentry. Kingsley was the third son of Nathan Kingsley of New Milford, Connecticut.[234] Because he didn't reveal it in his diary, his age is unclear. On Thursday, February 8, 1849, after a final visit to New Preston, Connecticut, to see his family and friends, Nelson Kingsley arrived in New Haven. He was a member of a company that he noted in his journal as The New Haven and California Joint Stock Company. This company's board of directors held meetings before the group set sail from Connecticut. These meetings continued occasionally to be held, even in the gold fields of northern California, from late in 1849 throughout much of 1850. Other miners in this book, also in the early stages of their journeys, sometimes were members of other so-called companies that began

---

[234] Both New Milford and New Preston are in western Connecticut within Litchfield County.

as the adventurers left home, but this was the only company that continued intact once the gold seekers actually reached the gold regions.

Although he attended some early board meetings, Kingsley wasn't a director. Because placer mining was a very risky business, the company did not survive the entire gold rush. On February 18, 1851, discouraged and no longer hopeful of striking it rich, Kingsley sold his claim for two hundred dollars. He resigned his company membership so that he might return to his former life in western Connecticut. He wanted to return to marry his fiancée, Miss E. W. She was never far from his mind throughout his whole time as a gold seeker.

He was one of a total party of sixty adventurers, each of whom paid three hundred dollars for passage on a vessel sailing around Cape Horn bound for California. Their goal, like everyone in this book, was to find and extract a large amount of gold (a "pile") in order to be able to return home within a year or so and live in ease. It may have been on this last visit to New Preston that Kingsley became engaged to a young lady, Miss W. or Miss E. W. Wherever a letter could possibly be mailed, such as in a port (or if accepted by another ship at sea) or from a city near the mines, Kingsley would write a letter home to his sweetheart.

Kingsley possessed many skills as a builder. He not only did many repairs on the ship his company sailed on, the brig *Anna Reynolds*, but he also helped other members of his company build a steamboat on deck, to be used on California's rivers. In addition to his ability as a worker, he had social skills that helped him fit in well with other company employees, daughters of American port officials, foreigners, and members of the ship's crew. He loved to sing in church choirs or in choral groups. For a pastime, either on board ship, when in the Chilean port of Talcahuana, or during 1850 while taking a break from the monotony of mining, Kingsley reported in his diary taking the time to sing. In addition to his abilities as a builder and singer, he played the flute. He included this instrument along with his raincoat, sweaters, changes of clothes, and carpenter's toolbox in his sea chest when he boarded the *Anna Reynolds* on February 23, 1849.

Before Kingsley and the other prospective forty-niners set foot on the ship that they'd call home for the next nearly eight months, the group met in private to form The New Haven and California Joint Stock Company.

Although he was included in some preliminary meetings, like a young employee might well be in one of today's startup companies, Kingsley wasn't on salary. Neither were any of his coworkers, some of whose last names were recorded in his diary. In one early entry in the diary, Kingsley included his own name as a company director. About this same time, he bought himself a pistol. There is no entry in his diary regarding his ever firing it at anything. Each had paid a passage fee of three hundred dollars to eventually sail by way of the Cape Verdes Islands and the Falkland Islands around Cape Horn to San Francisco.

After another company meeting on March 8, Kingsley and Henry Potter were dispatched as a company committee to New Haven. They bought muskets "for $1.25 apiece at A. W. Spies No. 91 Maiden Lane."[235] Kingsley assisted others to build a structure he referred to as "the house" on deck and installed flooring of the ship's "forecastle." Captain Bottom strictly followed the port's regulations, which involved posting guards over crewmen who may have considered jumping ship.

The ship sailed on Monday, March 16. Many passengers, including many crewmembers, became extremely seasick in the rough seas of the North Atlantic. Perhaps if they had known the ship's complete course would take them out of their way to the Cape Verdes Isles, the Falkland Islands, and Talcahuano, Chile, company members might have retched even more. At the end of each daily entry in his diary, Kingsley noted the wind direction and speed, as well as longitude and latitude. On April 6, the carpenter noted the first unusual event during the first half of their voyage. After being at sea for almost one month,

> an Austrain" [Austrian or Australian?] approached the ship but did not speak [to] her as she seemed scared at our red shirts, on which our Cap'n got us out with muskets and drums, on which she altered her course, and was soon out of sight.[236]

---

[235] Nelson Kingsley, *Diary of Nelson Kingsley, A California Argonaut of 1849,* Frederick J. Teggert, Editor, (Berkeley, CA, University of California Press, 1914), p. 241.

[236] *Ibid.,* Mr. Bottom was captain during the first part of the voyage until the brig docked for repairs in southern Chile. When the *Anna Reynolds* left Chile to sail to San Francisco, Mr. Webb, the first mate, replaced Mr. Bottom at the helm.

A few days later, on April 9, another member of Kingsley's company, Mr. Jennings, nearly drowned after falling overboard. Partly because he was spotted and partly because Jennings was a strong swimmer, they rescued him.

After several days of rough seas, on April 13 an English ship approached the *Anna Reynolds*. Kingsley noted the following short exchange between the ship captains.

> Captain Bottom: "Ahoy! Where are you from?"
> English captain: "From England and Lisbon."
> Captain Bottom: "Where are you bound?"
> English captain: "To Tampico."
> Captain Bottom: "Do you want anything?"
> English captain: "No."
> Captain Bottom: "Will you allow us to come on board and send letters?"
> English captain: "Yes."[237]

The English ship had sailed from Liverpool. After North Atlantic storms dismasted it, the captain put in for repairs at Lisbon, Portugal. Captain Bottom supplied them with potatoes. Before returning to his ship, Captain Bottom bought "a few bottles [of] some choice wines."[238] Although such friendly contacts between foreign ships at sea didn't occur every day, this kind of contact was not unheard of. After meeting trade winds, they sped up so that by mid-April, they reached the Cape Verdes Islands.

On their thirty-sixth day at sea, April 21, Kingsley was taken aback by what appeared on the horizon.

> Land, plain to be seen St. Antonio—tho' at a distance, looked
> like clouds rising out of the sea, ran in very near and saw men
> in boats comeing [coming] toward us—Most splendid scene, she
> looked like a barren rocky mass rising far above the clouds ...

---

[237] *Ibid.*, p. 242.

[238] *Ibid.*, p. 243. Kingsley noted that the *Anna Reynolds* outsailed the English ship as they separated.

saw a schooner comeing [coming] down before the wind came near and spoke [to her] she was loaded with passengers for California.[239]

After the brig anchored in San Antonio Bay, Kingsley went ashore to get his laundry done. He wrote, "the female portion seem to be led to prostitution especially by ships comeing [coming] in and stopping here."[240] He noted that customs on these islands weren't the same as in Connecticut. "The evil is not felt here as in our own country."[241] Kingsley came ashore a couple of days later, where he and Mr. S. N. Norton visited the American consul's plantation and noted that he "wrote letters to our friends I wrote one to Miss W, one to my father, and one to John G. North."[242] Before returning to the ship, he had dinner with Captain Bottom.

During the rest of April and from May to August, they sailed in a southwestward direction across the Atlantic. Kingsley, along with members of the New Haven and California Joint Stock Company, worked on a number of projects such as making hats, tinkering with gold washing machines, and working on the steamboat on the deck of the *Anna Reynolds*. The weather was very hot. In June, they crossed the equator. When needed, they took breaks to cool off a little under an awning stretched out on the deck. On May 11, Kingsley wrote,

> most all kinds of business going on—some are muddleing [muddling] steam-boats some drilling bearings to washing machines—some braiding hats.[243]

Evenings and nights were boring. Their voyage seemed endless, as if it would never end. Their little vessel seemed to be dwarfed by the immensity of

---

[239] *Ibid.*, p. 246.

[240] *Ibid.*, p. 247.

[241] *Ibid.*, p. 247.

[242] *Ibid.*, p. 248. Probably because he had to write in his *Diary* when tired or in a hurry, Kingsley omitted punctuation marks at the end of sentences. He omitted capitals when starting new sentences.

[243] *Ibid.*, pp. 252-253.

the sea as the *Anna Reynolds* began crossing the broadest part of the southern Atlantic Ocean. While the captain and crew's time was taken up with keeping watch, trimming sails, and making needed course corrections, the passengers sought ways to pass the time, even to entertain themselves. One way was by debating certain subjects. One debate topic was, "Are early marriages conducive of the general good?"

During May and June, the passengers conducted more debates.

1. Was the manner in which our forefathers treated the Aborigines justifiable?
2. Will the discovery of gold in California be beneficial to the United States?
3. Which exercises a greater influence on the mind of mankind, wealth or women?
4. Are any of this company justified in private speculation?
5. Does the abolishment of capital punishment tend to crime?[244]

James P. Keeler was the chosen secretary for the debates. After lengthy discussions on each of these above topics, they voted. They didn't agree on a decision on the first or the fourth questions. In the third, they decided that wealth was more important influence on the mind of mankind than women were. In the second and last questions, their consensus was in the negative. This showed that although the company membership was important, at least in the early part of this expedition, there might come a time when private speculation would be acceptable. In particular, on the last question there was no consensus; this is a tough one on which most Americans may still not agree.

By the beginning of August, they'd already been at sea for five months. Their tedious voyage had begun to wear them down, On August 6 at about two o'clock in the afternoon, they sighted land.

> At dark we made into a fine bay near the south part of one of the West Falkland named Queen Charlotte's Bay. As we enter the

---

[244] *Ibid.,* pp. 253-255.

bay from the west there is a small island at the left. It is covered with a small shrubby bog called tussock.[245]

Early the next day, in a gale force wind, the captain and a hunting party went ashore. At noon, they returned to the ship with "42 geese, 11 ducks, 1 hair [hare], 1 seal, 1 prairie wolf."[246]

The ship had passed over a large portion of the earth. They had sailed from New Haven, Connecticut, to the Cape Verdes Islands, a distance of 3,405 miles. Next, from Cape Verdes to the Falkland Islands, the *Anna Reynolds* had traveled 4,342 miles (8,373 kilometers). They had not even gone halfway—7,500 miles of ocean travel lay ahead.

Six days after arriving at the Falkland Islands, Kingsley, the homesick Yankee, wrote,

> I should like to see home now and catch a smell of new mown hay, and ripe harvest, and enjoy some of the ripe fruits which are now comeing [coming] on there, and be among my friends, but I must be content with that which I have thrown myself into with will I shall soon see warm weather again and then throw off this dull feeling which at times comes over me in spite of all exertion to the contrary.[247]

On August 13, he spotted another ship. Her colors proved her to be an American bark, the *Smyrna*, from New York. The ship had sailed May 15, making a stop at Rio. When Captain Bottom went on board the *Smyrna*, he discovered it carried lumber and California-bound passengers.

On Friday, August 17, the *Anna Reynolds* began encountering very rough seas. They were nearing Cape Horn. They had heard many stories of shipwrecks in attempts to sail around Cape Horn. Most of the passengers were only seen at mealtime; they spent much of their time in their berths. Kingsley wrote,

---

[245] *Ibid.,* p. 278. Tusssuck is a dense clump or tuft of grass.
[246] *Ibid.,* p. 279.
[247] *Ibid.,* p. 282.

It is tedious to day and no mistake as fast as the spray comes aboard it freezes and as we have no fire a good portion of us take to our berths and are seen only at meals, and not then unless we have something extra to eat, it is the best place after all for those that are not actually needed to work ship ... blew a gale all night.[248]

Two days later, on Sunday, August 19, he wrote, "This noon we was [were] some two degrees south of the Horn." He added, "Decks are all ice and one of the water casks are [is] froze up and things are generally in rather hard condition."[249]

On August 20, while performing his duty, a sailor's hands were frozen. A thick coat of ice had formed on deck, which had to be laboriously cracked. Kingsley remarked with chagrin, "I have heard many stories about the terrors of Cape Horn, but it is more interesting to hear stories about it, than to enjoy the realities."[250] The diarist continued by pining for his home,

> Tremendous waves come towards us as if to swallow us up immediately but it is surprising to see them as it were to die away as the vessel mounts them[.] This afternoon at 2 oclock [o'clock] Captain says we are in the exact Longitude as far as of New Haven, and for my part could almost wish myself in the same
>
> Latitude ... but such is life, and this must count, 'as all in my life time' so I shall let it pass as that.[251]

Two days after rounding Cape Horn, as the ship's course was set northward, they experienced a gale at night. "It blew everything all out straight, and while they were putting the last reef to the main top sail, the yard broke in

---

[248] *Ibid.*, p. 284.
[249] *Ibid.*, p. 285.
[250] *Ibid.*, p. 285.
[251] *Ibid.*, p. 285.

the middle.[252] This was a serious situation because the heavy waves continued to break over the starboard bow. Fear crept in because they were in serious trouble for the first time in the voyage.

Over the next two days, as they finished erecting replacement sails, they crossed course with an English ship, the *Sir Robert Peel*. Crewmen aboard this ship reported they had taken three weeks to successfully navigate around Cape Horn "when our time has been much shorter."[253] Although the *Anna Reynolds* had entered the southern Pacific Ocean, they encountered rough seas, huge waves, and high winds, especially at night. The captain of the English vessel told them about another American ship out of Portland, Maine. This vessel carried one hundred Americans bound for California. It tried three times to get around Cape Horn but had had to return to Montevideo, Uruguay, for repairs.

On September 7, they sailed close and parallel to a slow-moving Swedish ship, the *Charles Quint D'Ampers*. It had taken sixty days for this ship to sail around the Horn from Rio to their current position, approximately fifty miles off the coast of South America.

> We had a fine talk sailing parallel for a short time. Both ships saluted each other with 3 cheers and rang her bell quite merrily for a while ... Held another prayer service, headed in towards south coast of Chile.[254]

The *Anna Reynolds* changed course, now heading north by northeast. On September 14, they entered the port of Talcahuano, a town close to Concepcio'n, Chile. After constructing a rope ladder to be used for boarding lorries, on September 15 Kingsley went on shore. While the ship was being repaired, the company members, including Kingsley, remained in port until October 2. Mr. Kingsley would soon be blessed with a very pleasant time, meeting some beautiful young ladies and enjoying their families' warm Chilean hospitality. The young American man walked about the town discovering that, although

---

[252] *Ibid.*, p. 286.

[253] *Ibid.*, p. 288.

[254] *Ibid.*, p. 292.

most of the people were "Spanish," there also were some "Americans and English."[255]

After spending one night at the Commercial Hotel, Kingsley encountered

> a gentleman and two or three Ladies' riding in an ox cart. Arriving in town I found one of the Ladies to be a beautiful player on the Piano Forte, whose father (miser-like) has gone to California, which I suppose made them more interested in me as they are to send letters to him by me.[256]

On September 18, another American bark, the *Hannah Sprague,* came into Talcahuana from New York with 120 passengers on board also bound for California. The small town was beginning to fill as two more vessels, the *Canada* with six passengers out of New Bedford and an English tender, arrived.

Three days later, on September 21, Kingsley and nine others from New Haven sailed a whale boat across the harbor to a small place called Pinco. Here was a big flour mill producing forty bushels of flour per day. Writing in his diary, Kingsley predicted that this part of South America would soon "yield large quantities of wheat for exportation." During the early years of the Gold Rush, a great many barrels of Chilean flour sustained the burgeoning population of California. On Saturday, September 22, another ship, the *Chili,* arrived. Later that day, he witnessed the burial of a child. On Sunday, he

> Tuned and put in two new strings of a Piano Forte for the Captain of the Port [Mr. Williams] whose daughter is a very fine player That PM was invited to an Englishman's [Mr. Neisbits] who is working the coal mines here, gave him a specimen of our music. Said he "never enjoyed an evening so well in his life." He had two beautiful daughters together with other young ladies which were dressed very rich, and handsome.[257]

---

[255] *Ibid.,* p. 293.
[256] *Ibid.,* p. 295 and 298.
[257] *Ibid.,* pp. 300-301.

The flour mill's manager was Mr. Lewis, originally from Bridgeport, Connecticut. His salary was $1,500 a year. This was an excellent salary for a comparable position anywhere in the world in1849. In addition to the wheat and flour business, the town had built and soon would ship "six hundred small frame buildings of about 14 by 18 to San Francisco." Lumber had been so scarce in San Francisco before 1850 that for a short period, builders as far away as New York State and South America were shipping this kind of prefabricated house to San Francisco. Kingsley noted that a good carpenter and joiner could get three dollars per day, "and some get more."[258]

By September 27, some of Kingsley's fellow passengers were becoming anxious to get underway. Everyone knew that during the nearly six months since they'd sailed from New England, miners in the California gold regions were finding many rich gold deposits.

---

[258] *Ibid.,* p. 301.

CHAPTER 8

Nelson Kingsley: The End of the Voyage

While watching large gray swells of the Pacific Ocean from the bow of the ship, Kingsley was relieved to at last be underway again. Just after they finally sailed from Talcahuano at the end of September, another ship, the *Nahum Keag,* followed the *Anna Reynolds* out to sea. Meanwhile, there had been a reorganization of the ship's crew. A new captain, Mr. Webb, replaced Mr. Bottom. Webb, who stepped up from first mate, at first got along better with the other crew members. Also within the New Haven and California Joint Stock Company's managers, there was a shift in positions so that each member had a new job to do. Some went to work on the new steamboat being built on deck. Others continued making hats or working on the washing machines to be used to separate gold from dirt once they got to the mining district.

The waves were so large that as they headed north, the new passengers who had boarded in Chile got seasick. Kingsley spent the early part of one day attending to his tools so they would be ready for use when he needed them. The passengers and some of the crew held a Sunday meeting on deck, and a sermon was read by a "Cap'n Ford," which Kingsley found interesting.

> To-day is a day that is well callculated [calculated] to lead our thoughts away to those friends we have left behind and renews an anxiety to get to a place we can hear from them but no doubt they (are) as anxious about us ... but here we are safe as it were, gliding up the pacific at the rate of 9 knots per hour ... and may be prospered speedily and allowed to return home, which will be the happiest day in my life. A new bird called the Booby has

made his appearance to day, it is very like the albatross but now
large with a straight awkward bill.[259]

As he often did in his diary, Kingsley took the time to think about his friends
at home in Connecticut. At the same time, he made daily comments about the
weather, noting in this passage the temperature rose as they approached the
equator.

As the *Anna Reynolds* continued its solitary voyage toward San Francisco,
many trades were pursued on board as October passed. Unlike modern cruise
ship passengers, each member of Kingsley's company had a job to accomplish.
The machinist, Mr. Ellis, worked to prepare engines while Mr. Stuart made
tents. The blacksmith hammered away at "iron work for the boat." Kingsley
worked "at rabbeting the stern piece to the steamboat." On October 9, he wrote,

> One cask of our beautiful dried peaches was dumped overboard
> to day because we thought the cask worth more for other uses
> Mr. Stuart commenced the tents to day which are yet to be
> finished[.] This afternoon we saw a sail but she was bound the
> other way and was soon out of sight-We drawed for berths
> this evening which is the last time I shall take my hammock
> after this, much anxiety now exists throughout the company
> to arrive at our journeys end as it seems the nearer we get
> to it the more interest is excited among us, the general news
> recieved [received] at the last port respecting the gold, and
> the impatience to hear from our friends at home leads us to
> anticipate it with interest Course NW by W, Lat 21 degrees 47'
> Lon 83 degrees 32 1/2'.[260]

On October 16, they "passed under the latitude of the sun to day makeing
[making] it overhead at noon. I think it will be a long time before I see it
north of me again, and more likely never."[261] Anxiety along with boredom had

---

259 *Ibid.*, pp. 304-305.
260 *Ibid.*, p. 306.
261 *Ibid.*, p. 307.

brought him to the point of feeling almost fatalistic. Just as it would later do after his company reached the mines, doing each day's work brought him out of his doldrums. He had to help "Mr Brockett on the Figure-head ... Mr Barber is getting up brands and stamps to designat [designate] for our companys [company's] name."[262]

On October 29, "Last night the boys caught a purpass [porpoise] ... Finished the joint to my flute, and it proved to be verry [very] perfect in tone which was proved by trying it with Mr Spencer."[263] Kingsley hadn't lost his passion for music or to play a role, whether by playing his flute or by singing. Also, his carpentry was being utilized.

Throughout the first two weeks of November, the ship sailed northwestward until it was only a few days from reaching its destination. On Saturday, November 17, he wrote,

> We tacked ship light wind, this morning we saw a sail to the westward, we set our colors, towards noon we found her to be what we thought to be what we thought a Sweed [Swede, or a Swedish ship] bound on the same course as ourselves, help the Cap work out a lunar this evening from Saturn and the moon.

There seemed to be nothing to fear. However, the sailors assigned the watch during the early morning hours of November 18 didn't see the oncoming vessel, the Swedish ship which Kingsley had noted above. As a result of poor surveillance, the Swedish ship, ironically named *America*, smashed into the *Anna Reynolds* just a few yards from its bow. Fortunately for all on board the *Anna Reynolds*, the *America* was moving slowly when the two vessels collided.

> This morning about 1/2 past 2 oclock [o'clock], we tacked ship and stood North, with prospects of the wind fair which sprung up from the west About 3 oclock [o'clock] we were all awoke by a tremendous crash forward as if every splinter that could be broken loose from us was about to be severed, I sprung out,

---

[262] *Ibid.,* p. 308.

[263] *Ibid.,* p. 312.

and found that the ship we saw yesterday was upon our decks crushing our bulwarks in a terrible manner, with her bow, at every surge of the sea.[264]

Several times later in his diary, Kingsley referred to the good luck they'd enjoyed that early November morning by having a light wind instead of much stronger winds and rapid currents. Otherwise, their ship might have sprung a leak or broken in two and sunk, with the drowning of all or many on board.

Four days later, on the afternoon of November 22, they sailed into San Francisco Bay. At last, their more than eight-month long voyage ended. On the next day, November 23, they set foot on California soil, and he recorded his initial impression.

> For my part must confess this is a *great country* for there is [are] people almost without number, and looks like a town meeting or general Training. The place consists of any thing for a house, and any quantity of tents pitched in the vicinity of the village. The town lies on a side hill [on the side of a hill] and it is beyond anything I ever thought, and almost baffles description and can give but a faint idea concerning it.[265]

Just as the city can sometimes seem strange to first-time visitors today, San Francisco looked to him to be only a "village" on some windswept "hillside." It was surrounded by tents. Although Kingsley was unaware of it, already San Francisco had been surveyed and a map made and published by a professional cartographer, Jasper O'Farrell.[266] Kingsley noted how a few individuals made small fires "with sticks, a teakettle trying to make it boil."[267] Furthermore. "all

---

[264] *Ibid.,* p. 316.

[265] *Ibid.,* p. 320.

[266] *Ibid.,* See O'Farrell's biography, Frank Baumgardner, *Blood will Tell Divvying Up Early California from Colonel Juan Bautista De Anza to Jasper O'Farrell,* North Charleston, SC, CreateSpace Independent Publishing Platform, 2014), Chapter Six.

[267] *Ibid.,* p 320. This may have been tempting to him, but he had committed himself to his company and coworkers.

seems like confusion and the place looks like a thing built for the present ...
merely stuck up temporarily the quickest way possible." Getting a bit more
specific, he continued. "Joiners get at present 13 dollars and much more
in summer or anything they are disposed to ask."[268] If he was tempted at
all to desert his coworkers getting ready to go to Sacramento and the gold
fields to work as a carpenter in San Francisco, Kingsley didn't mention it.
"Board is from 16 to 25 dollars per week." Everything seemed costly to him.
For example, "One of our fellows was offered 50 dollars for his books." On
Saturday, November 24, he remained on board in the morning writing "some
letters for home." Along with others, he visited another ship, the *Anna Smith,*
"and had a chat."[269]

Later the same day, he went on shore. He reported,

> It almost baffles description[.] Gambling seems to be the only
> business that attracts attention. If I was in possession of one
> half the coin and dust I have seen to night I could start for home
> immediately, and woe to the poor D____ls who are so foolish as
> to haunt these places.[270]

Having no gold dust and apparently not much money, Kingsley was not in
danger of losing a lot in the gambling halls. Partly because it was the rainy
season, the casinos thronged with willing miners who quickly lost their hard-
earned gains at the monte, poker, or roulette tables.

On Sunday, November 25, he

> attended church. The Episcopal church is built on a little
> eminence overlooking part of the city and the Harbor[.] the
> building is 18 × 50 feet and cost $10,000, ground and all and is
> only framed and clap-boarded & roofed with cloth. Mr Mines
> the minister is an excellent preacher, and a good congregation

---

[268] *Ibid.,* p. 320.

[269] *Ibid,.* p. 320.

[270] *Ibid.,* p. 320

to listen I visited the office of Mr. Hoadley from Plymouth Ct. [Plymouth City, Massachusetts] who is engaged as a surveyor.[271]

On November 27, they set out across the bay for Sacramento. As was the case earlier that month when the *Anna Reynolds* had collided with the *America*, bad luck returned. Again they were struck by another vessel, this time while in San Pablo Bay, the north part of San Francisco Bay. In the accident, they nearly lost their "Main-Yard." This time the damage to the ship was more serious, including a broken "head gear and the removal of the bowsprit." They fished out the "Main-Yard."[272] Kingsley also noted that the currents were very swift as they approached Benicia.

During the next day, they progressed northeastward, going up the Sacramento River. Their ship wasn't the only oceangoing ship that sailed inland onto the rivers of northern California. As we shall see, they would have contact with other oceangoing ships, such as the *Sea Witch*, a small schooner which carried Edward Chever to San Francisco. On November 29, Kingsley noted,

> After getting up four or five miles we passed the Schooner *Friendship*[.] all well ... the soil appears rich and the air salubrious, quantities of wild geese are seen flying over and around us, but not one has been shot by our crowd yet ... the days a verry [very] warm like a New England September, but the nights are cold To day has been appointed as a day of thanksgiving here, but my supper consisted of beans old hoss and hard bread.[273]

He estimated they had gone fifteen miles upriver on November 29. During the following month, the Grim Reaper was busy. In December, three members of Mr. Kingsley's company died. Although others still alive were suffering from scurvy or dysentery, now his company faced a hard choice: remain huddled in tents along the Sacramento River below Sacramento, or attempt going on up to the mines as soon as possible.

---

[271] *Ibid.*, p. 321.

[272] *Ibid.*, p. 321.

[273] *Ibid.*, p. 322.

The passings of company members did not affect Kingsley right away because he made no more note in his diary of anyone else who died or was very ill. Although this was the first time there was a serious decision to make, where there may have been a significant difference of opinion, a majority decided to wait to begin serious mining until spring. California's annual heavy rainy season was underway with nearly constant rain throughout the nights. On December 1, Kingsley noted,

> Some of us went ashore last night and killed 6 geese, there are any quantity flying around and over us game seems to be verry [very] plenty but exceedingly wild. The banks are more dry as we get farther up, and abound with a sort of oak resembling live oak, some of us went ashore and cut boat loads which will be valuable on arriving at Sacramento.[274]

Whereas other forty-niners continued working at bringing in loads of wood for Sacramento residents and others to burn, Kingsley's company didn't continue working in this way because the pay at fifteen dollars a cord wasn't sufficient for the labor involved. Still on board their ship, the *Anna Reynolds*, the company was caught in a "slough"[275] and experienced high winds that made controlling the ship difficult. On December 3, Kingsley wrote, "Had a severe turn of the diarrhea last night."[276]

Despite feeling bad, he was thankful for a good tent that afforded him shelter and comfort.

> Wind ahead strong all day and have kept ourselves comfortable in company with other schooners waiting for a fair wind, 5 of our company starting for Sacramento City to see Mr. Smith, built a smashing fire on shore and in the afternoon got out a ridge pole for a tent and pitched one to see how it would look

---

[274] *Ibid.*, p. 323.
[275] *Ibid.*, p. 323.
[276] *Ibid.*, p. 323.

and I have seen none that looks more comfortable as they are
large and spacious.[277]

The young carpenter appreciated Mr. Stuart's tent making work. Their
company was well organized. Their tents seemed better to him than many
that others had.

Soon after this, there was another board meeting, which Kingsley attended.
It set up another hierarchy of command.

> For the coming year Messrs. Henry G. Smith 1st director Henry
> Potter 2nd James Stuart 3d Wm Whipple 4th John Ayer 5th P
> Brockett 6th directors James P Keeler Secretary, H. O. McCoy
> Treasurer.[278]

They also discussed how any profits might be distributed, including to
shareholders back home, but Kingsley doubted that much would ever be
returned. "We also appointed five as a judicial committee to investigate cases
of disorderly conduct of any member."[279]

During December 8–10, they headed upriver to Sacramento. On December 9,

> Found ourselves in a city of tents, some not as good as the one
> we had and should have supposed myself in an extraordinary
> large camp meeting had I not known to the contrary I strolled
> out in the morning and gave $1.25 for 3 pound of fresh beef
> this seemed mighty big but we shall soon get used to California
> prices.[280]

On December 12, Kingsley was grateful to be shielded from the rain because
he "set a tent on shore and put a stove in it and made things quite comfortable
for a rainy day."[281]

---

[277] *Ibid.*, p. 323.
[278] *Ibid.*, p. 324.
[279] *Ibid.*, p. 324.
[280] *Ibid.*, p. 324.
[281] *Ibid.*, p. 326.

As 1850 began, he returned to carpentry. On New Year's Day, rain continued to fall. In the meantime, more members of the company had fallen ill.

> Worked on the scow a little. We moved the sick ashore into the *Senate* which we have laid a floor in and made very comfortable for a hospital. Our sickest is Arthur W[.] Seeley he has the dysentery bad and very sore mouth Mr W Welton is about the sam [same] Mr Stuart some better Mr Hobart was taken yesterday and is quite down today Mr. Spencer was quite sick yesterday but feel better ... Apart from this we are generally well but there are but few that say they can do as much in a day as when they left home.[282]

As is still true today, New Year's Day was a day of reflection as well as planning. On this first day of his newfound life on the banks of the Sacramento River in 1850, Kingsley expressed his longing for home in a poem that began with the word "Home."

> Home, that sweetest if all words,
> Hath charms without disguise;
> It is the place that hath no odds,
> For mortal man below the skies.
> Tis there, where manhood first begins;
> Tis there, true hapiness [happiness] is found;
> The many troubles seem to reign
> Yet home's the place where comfort's always found
>
> But where we grow to riper years;
> We seek for wealth in foreign lands,
> Our fondest friends we leave in tears
> To *serve Ambitions* [italics Mr. Kingsley's] selfish ends

---

[282] *Ibid.*, p. 329. The *Senate* was acknowledged by many as being one the best steamboats in regular operation on the Sacramento River from San Francisco to Sacramento.

My dearest friend I'll think of thee
While in a land so far away
Hoping (though I must bear the sea)
My welcome there some future day.[283]

Although Kingsley failed here to add her initials in his diary, there can be little doubt that "my dearest friend" was Miss E. W., the Connecticut young lady, to whom he was engaged and yearned to return to.

On January 8, he reported having a birthday. He also wrote some "letters for home" that he planned to send back to San Francisco on the bark. On January 9, he noted,

Mr Arthur W Seely [Seeley] died this morning about 5 oclock [o'clock] … abuut 5 oclock [o'clock] this afternoon his funeral, after which we took him down the river about one mile and a half, and buried him in an Indian Mound which is a much better place than I expected could be found about here, his burial was executed the best that circumstances would allow, he had a very decent coffin and a dry place for the grave, several bones of those that had been buried there were dug up and a pestle and some little round stones, from this we supposed that it must have been a squaw as it is the custom among the Indians to bury the implements to which the individual was accustomed to along with them … Mr Seely was verry [very] patient, and endureing [enduring] and until a day or two previous to his death was perfectly sensible of all that took place around him, even to the smallest grain of medicine. … He would often while in the room with 3 others that were sick crack many a dry and witty joke and make many pithy remarks.[284]

---

[283] Ibid., 320.

[284] *Ibid,"* p. 332–333. Immigrants to California sometimes used Indians' "squaws" for pleasurable, intimate moments and their sacred places for burial grounds when a white died.

Kingsley's carpentry skills were almost constantly in demand. On January 11, he wrote,

> This morning the scow was launched and the Bark started down at a good rate with the current, I went to work on the steamboat, laid down the kelson [or keelson][285] and set the timbers spiked on the bottom ... sent down the letters by Mr. Smith.[286]

Their party was still adjusting to life in rough-and-tumble northern California. It began sinking in that getting rich wasn't going to be quick or come easy. In fact, simply to survive would be an accomplishment. More of their party would die before long. On January 26, Kingsley recorded,

> A boat came down the river with four men in it going on a hunting excursion one of which had been in the mines on the Yuba. He gave flattering accounts of the gold in that region at the same time allowing that it is work to get the gold. ... set up a "pit-saw," Some half a dozen standing around looking at us & laughing, I suppose that could do better.[287]

Although nobody likes to be made fun of, if he minded being ribbed a little by others, Kingsley didn't show it. Because he knew his party were greenhorns, he didn't want to show embarrassment in front of the other, more weathered veteran forty-niners.

The rains continued unabatedly. More of his coworkers got sick. In part at least, their declines in health were due to exposure to the elements. On January 26, Kingsley noted,

---

[285] *Ibid*, p. 333. *Kelson* is a variant spelling of the word *keelson*. A keelson is defined as a "structure running the length of a ship that fastens the timber or plates of the floor to the keel." *Concise Oxford English Dictionary*, 11th edition, eds. Catherine Soanes and Angus Stevenson.

[286] *Ibid.*, p. 333. As noted earlier, Harry G. Smith was "1st Director" of the company. He was also a friend and mentor of Nelson Kingsley.

[287] *Ibid.*, p. 338.

The river is risen a little more and we are in the water. Mr Stuart
is very hard sick with dysentery but has symptoms of a recovery
many are poisoned very bad, and for ought I see, will continue
to be so during our stay here Lobellia is the great cure but some
are against it as the cure is not the same [on] one as on another.
(brackets Mr Kingsley's)[288]

As anyone who has ever gone camping during the winter in northern
California knows, the tent ground will get wet. Two days later, on January 28,
Edward Keeler died. Two days after this, news from a recently arrived boat
from San Francisco came of William H. Harrison's death

Many of Kingsley's company coworkers were depressed by the bad weather
and the illnesses and deaths of their friends. Company morale was breaking
down. Some elected to leave for the mines to strike out on their own. Some
even returned to Benicia. On March 6 at 4:00 p.m., Kingsley and his coworkers
weighed anchor on board the bark to embark for Sacramento. On Friday,
February 8, he noted,

The sch's [schooner] *Sea Witch* along-side of us last night and
this morning we have a fair wind and after breakfast got under
weigh [way] and was [were] in Sacramento about 12 oclock
[o'clock]. Business is now verry [very] brisk here, although it
has been dull for the last two months[.] New buildings are going
up all around and the shipping which line the bank and there
are large piles of lumber.[289]

During the next month, young Kingsley and a group of fellow New
Englanders reached the mines at a location "about twenty-five miles up the
American River." On March 14, Kingsley, continuing this notation above, wrote
as if he'd been caught performing a schoolboy's prank.

---

[288] *Ibid.,* p. 339. Lobelia is defined as a plant of the bellflower family; typically with blue or
scarlet flowers. Origin: Named after the Flemish botanist Mathias de Lobel [1538–1616]."
Concise Oxford English Dictionary, 11th edition, eds. Catherine Soanes and Angus Stevenson.
[289] *Ibid.,* p. 339.

Went down and set our rocker and began to do the same as the rest around us were doing found the shiny stuff was 'dur' [dear or dull?] but not very plenty, the business seemed like a new way to make money, and should one of our Eastern Mothers see one of their boys doing a thing that looks as simple & foolish as this they *would give them a whipping,* and send them in the house.[290]

Two other members of his company went upriver four miles to the diggings at Mormon Island. At first, Kingsley decided to stay put. On Saturday, March 23, he "wrote a letter home and done very well got about 25 dollars worth which is better than the average at the present time."[291] This was the first actual gold he had ever removed from California soil. Kingsley may have ended the day with a feeling of accomplishment because it was exactly one year and a week after their vessel, the bark *Anna Reynolds,* had set sail, bound for San Francisco. Following the two members of his company mentioned earlier, Kingsley also moved on to Mormon Island. On March 26, he "took out about 20 dollars but shall have to give it up on account of water."[292] Two days later, he received news of a significant change in the company that he and his cohorts had been part of so far.

> Messrs Whipple, Taft, Spencer and McCoy arrived here to day and bring news that the Joint Stock Co' have [has] come to a close, and everything is about being sold & settling up as fast as possible, and leaves every member to do for a livelihood that which seems best. The famous Steamboat *Etna* was sold under the hammer at 5200 dollars people gave us the praise of a pretty moddle [model] which reflects a little credit on its builders.[293]

Although this wasn't the last contact Kingsley would have with the company, it was unsettling news. As one of the builders of the steamboat,

---

[290] *Ibid.,* p. 348.
[291] *Ibid.,* p. 349.
[292] *Ibid.,* p. 349.
[293] *Ibid.,* p. 351.

Kingsley may have justifiably felt like he was getting a raw deal because this turn of events meant he would not be paid for the hours of carpentry he'd put in to construct this vessel. If he was cheated out of some payment, he could have lawfully felt he was due; certainly he wasn't alone. Such things happened to many other immigrants who were part of California's great gold rush.

On April 3, he and a coworker were "on the bar [probably back on what they called "Nigger Bar"] and near Mormons Island in our old place and two of us got 24–45 which is better than our average."[294] With a decrease in heavy rain, in general things were improving for the miners. Friday, April 5, was a special day.

> Mr Geo' [Mr. George] Hotchkiss came up today and brought me a
> letter from home dated the 16 & 17 of Jan [January], which was
> a rich feast for me as it is the first since June from E W.[295]

No doubt this was an exciting time for the carpenter. His future wife had sent him a letter, which had gotten to him in nearly record time. In addition to that, on Saturday, April 6, after he did his laundry, "We weighed our Gold and found we had 307 dollars." When added to what "we have paid away makes $356.49."[296]

Temporarily, at least, they were through with placer mining on the American River. Kingsley needed a break. His skills as a carpenter allowed him to earn some supplemental income doing other jobs besides mining. He decided to return to "Sacramento City and stay a spell," and "if Joiners business [the demand for carpenters] is good to work at my trade if not to go on the Yuba as soon as the water gets down."[297]

---

[294] *Ibid.,* p. 351. Because he wasn't specific here, probably Kingsley was still working at an American River site some referred to as "Nigger's Bar" by the whites. On October 3, 2019, an online search through the Google search engine revealed Elizabeth T. Knochs' MA thesis, *A Study of Place Names in the American River Drainage System, 1848-1854,* showed no such place name in the author's appendix. There was a "Nigger's Bluff, Placer County, near Folsom," p. 89.

[295] *Ibid.,* p. 351. Miss E. W.'s letter took approximately two and a half months to reach Kingsley from Connecticut to the California gold mines. For anyone who has ever been in love it is impossible to overemphacize the positive effect getting this letter from his beloved surely must have had on Kingsley.

[296] *Ibid.,* p. 351.

[297] *Ibid.,* p. 351.

Although the amount of gold he'd mined was certainly not as much as he'd dreamed of getting when he was back in New Preston, Connecticut, reading in newspapers about the rich finds others had made out west in California, his take for the spring of 1850 was good enough to keep his hopes alive.

When Kingsley and his coworkers got back to Sacramento, much of the city was still underwater. He "went to work as a carpenter for Messrs. Scranton & Smith at putting addition on their store"[298] on Monday, April 15. On April 19, he "sorted some stuff out of the pile of lumber and sawed up stuff for six rockers."[299] On the same day, he went back up to the bar to get some equipment he needed, and as he was on his way back to Sacramento, on April 18 he "heard of Mrs. Houser's death on the road down ... got down about 3 ocl.k [o'clock].[300]

In spite of being afflicted at least one day by "diarrhea," he spent Sunday, April 21, writing

> a letter to Marble Dale. The greatest sport I have had in California was last night.... Mr Smith & myself rowed upriver with a net.... we got 20 [fish] ... they made up the number of 51 salmon making a little over 1,000 lbs or half a ton of solid fish, the prettiest sight I ever saw in the fish line was this, they sell readily at 50 cts pr pound.[301]

Like many other forty-niners (including Samuel McNeil), Nelson Kingsley may not have gotten rich mining for gold, but he wasn't going broke either. After Kingsley put together a box, Mr. Smith took it with the fish down to San Francisco on board the *Senator*. Still in Sacramento while recovering from diarrhea, he "sawed out stuff for six rockers but have not worked verry ["very"] hard."[302]

Kingsley wrote another letter home. Getting it there wasn't always possible. On Thursday, April 25, a man who stayed the night with Kingsley, Julius Bassett

---

[298] *Ibid.*, p. 352.

[299] *Ibid.*, p. 352.

[300] *Ibid.*, p. 352.

[301] *Ibid.*, p. 353.

[302] *Ibid.*, p. 353.

of Humphreysville, Connecticut, agreed to carry his letter home for him. On Sunday, April 28, Kingsley "heard of a man being shot at Morman Island, in trying to extract the contents of a safe."[303] It wasn't the only violent incident; earlier, two men were badly cut in a drunken barroom fight.

On May 1, while Kingsley worked at Mr. Baldwin's in Sacramento,

> Mr Hubbard came down from the Yuba last night and report Mr Potter's crowd well except Mr. E. Ayer who is considerable [considerably] ill at present went up town and bought some screws & sheet iron for riddles and paid 11/4 dollars for screws pr gross and .50 cts [cents] pr 1 lbs for damaged sheet iron.[304]

Kingsley continued to produce rockers, which he could use later or sell to other miners. He took the evening off to attend the "Rowes Olympic Circus at the 'New Pacific Circus.'" Both Rowe and his wife were "splendid riders." He added, "The whole Troupe came up on the ship *Tusso* from Panama."[305]

On Saturday, May 11, Kingsley, Mr. Smith, and Mr. Summers traveled through "the little town of Nichaloss [Nicholaus] to Eliza where they spent the night. They had to find and hire a team to carry their things along."[306]

On May 6, he "sold two of the rockers for 46 dollars." Three days later, he finished a "quicksilver machine" he'd been working on. "Messrs Norton & Pearl arrived from San Francisco to day and brought a couple of letters for me one from E W and from Le Raysville CP Lines both gave me great satisfaction."[307] He also mentioned that he had had to work as quickly as he could in order to leave Sacramento to escape having to pay a "new levee put on vessels leaving Sacramento to go upriver."[308]

After his two companions went on ahead of him, Kingsley took charge of moving their goods, which required hiring one wagon. But the wagon had

---

[303] *Ibid.,* p. 353.

[304] *Ibid.,* p. 354.

[305] *Ibid.,* p. 354.

[306] *Ibid.,* p. 354.

[307] *Ibid.,* p. 355.

[308] *Ibid.,* p. 355.

a problem: it broke down on the road. He had to spend the night at another town, Carrell, while he awaited another wagon to arrive. He hired that wagon, which moved the goods into a "blue tent at Cordua." On Thursday, May 16, "Smith and Potter came down from Union Bar." Kingsley wrote, "Smith has bought a claim in their daming [damming] operation there ..." Smith "was appointed President of the company yesterday[.] Worked in the ravine above with a common rocker."[309]

On Friday, May 17, Kingsley wrote that he

> stoped [stopped] down to day and make a panning trough to pour quicksilver from the riffler[310] into and fix [fixed] the *Kingsley*, with many valuables and trinkets for the Indian trade had to work hard to save Baldwin's tent we should have saved more things but there were loaded guns, pistols & a keg of powder and all went off but did not injure any one.[311]

On Saturday, May 18. Kingsley wrote, "A cool but a fine day went over in the ravine and help [helped] on the Quicksilver Machine and had about 25 dolls [dollars] for my share."[312]

Now, together with six others, Kingsley resumed working their previous claim. On May 26, he noted making "a dividend of 65 dollars."[313] On the following day, May 27, an unusual thing happened.

> About 200 Indians & squaws came down and began to pan all around us, and dug the dirt with their hands, or sticks old pieces

---

[309] *Ibid.*, p. 356.

[310] A riffler is "an elongated tool for filing concave surfaces." *Concise Oxford English Dictionary*, 11th edition, eds. Catherine Soanes and Angus Stevenson.

[311] *Ibid.*, p. 356. Accidents, like this one apparently near or in the small town of Cordua, were almost everyday disasters in the mining districts. The forty-niners, like Kingsley and others in this study, developed a kind of brave nonchalance or bravado in order to save their sanity and continue to mine.

[312] *Ibid.*, p. 356.

[313] *Ibid.*, p. 357.

of iron and such like seemed to be verry [very] friendly and behaved verry [very] well.[314]

Kingsley's diary contains no other entries regarding Indian miners. Although none of Kingsley's party apparently did so, some whites employed groups of Indians to work the mines for them, paying them with food and/or a small portion of the gold extracted. On both May 28 and May 29, he "worked on the river." On May 29, he "got 10 1/2 oz of amalgam."[315]

As May gave way to June and while his personal pile grew a little, on June 3 his entry revealed much about one more informal reorganization that took place in the New Haven Joint Stock Company.

> The company met at noon and the stock and interest was transferred to me for which I am to give one thousand dollars in the fall if we do well[.] went to work in the race in the afternoon board with Norton's Co for a spell.[316]

Like a so-called penny stock today, Kingsley's company was always near bankruptcy. Obviously, though, Kingsley was a valued employee who could have done very well if the company should happen to really hit pay dirt.

On June 4, 1850, Kingsley "went to work rolling rocks out of the slue [slough]."

The site they worked at refilled with water each day. The daily schedule specified working for only seven hours a day with a break from ten until three.[317] There was another directors' meeting. The name of the company changed from the New Haven and California Joint Stock Company to the Union Association. Kingsley was one of fifteen other officers. He was about to strike out on his own.

On June 8, he left camp for Marysville to "buy provisions for the summer

---

[314] *Ibid.*, 357. Apparently an isolated happening. Kingsley made no other reference to such a large number of Indians, so it is unclear whether this group of Indians, who were almost certainly of the same tribe, were working for their own profit or were being employed by a white person.

[315] *Ibid.*, p. 357.

[316] *Ibid.*, p. 358.

[317] *Ibid.*, p. 358.

preparatory for living by myself." Upon reaching Marysville the next day, he "put up at the St. Louis Hotel kept by Mr Peak & lady from St. Louis," where he "finished up letters for home."[318]

As June ended, he continued working on the same site to build a new dam. On July 1, Kingsley found out that ne "was appointed to go down to Sacramento City to get stuff for making [making] our quicksilver machines.... Mr Smith, Foster, Kippen & myself started for sac' [Sacramento] city."[319] They arrived in Marysville, where he recorded temperatures as "105 shade, 124 sun ... started down at six oclock [o'clock] PM to Sac' [Sacramento] City on the *Gov [Governor] Dana*."[320]

After arriving in Sacramento in the evening, they stayed overnight at the Globe Hotel. On the next day, July 2, Kingsley and "Mr. Smith" were in for a big surprise because they

> made a visit up to where the bark lay in the American river[.] She looks rather hard compared to what the rest of the vessels do we went aboard found Dr Yale well but Mr Smith visited the safe where had been deposited som [some] four thousand dollars and on opening it found it gone, to his no small surprise & how could it be the safe well locked and he (Smith) in possession of the key and the other key he had carefully locked up in his trunk in his possession the next thing was to search the trunk no second key was to be found the the rascal had somehow picked the trunk lock & knowing the key to the safe was there, saw his way clear, we came to the conclusion that it was some one who knew how things were aboard the vessel and concluded to make the thing a secret untile [until] he could get some trace in the afternoon he started for San Francisco in the st'r [steamer?] *Gold Hunter.*[321]

---

318 *Ibid.,* p. 359. Kingsley continued working for many of the same coworkers.
319 *Ibid.,* p. 359.
320 *Ibid.,* pp. 359–361.
321 *Ibid.,* p. 362.

To Smith and Kingsley it seemed clear that William Keeler, who was the brother of the secretary who made notes of the company's debates on board the *Anna Reynolds,* was guilty. However, there was no conclusive evidence except for their own suppositions. In the meantime, the heat wave didn't let up. The temperature in Sacramento reached 104 in the shade. Kingsley had to assemble materials for more "machines except the frames."[322]

It wasn't long before the probable identity of the perpetrator of the robbery seemed clear to both Smith and Kingsley. On July 5, Kingsley wrote,

> Mr smith & Foster came in on the boat this morning Mr Smith has found verry [very] reliable information concerning the robbery & the guilt is now placed upon Mr Wm F Keeler who has remitted money home and has appeared to have plenty of money by him of late, he has left some time since for the Sandwich Islands [Hawaiian Islands] wither he said he was going to farming & should send for his family to meet him Circumstances are strongly against him and our suspicions must rest there until the truth is known to the contrary Finished picking out lumber to day to go up the river tomorrow.[323]

Frontier California had no modern police forces in 1850. Although it appeared almost certain to Kingsley and Mr. Smith from the circumstantial evidence, they had nothing on board the bark like crime investigational technique, such as fingerprinting or video camera footage, for example. Apparently, there had been no eyewitnesses. Their conclusion may not have been valid that the crime was committed by William Keeler. It could have been committed by someone else.

At the end of July, Kingsley returned to the Union Bar region to work. On Monday, July 29, he wrote,

---

[322] *Ibid.,* p. 262. Today Keeler might be termed a "person of interest," whose guilt or innocence would be determined by police at work, probably in California and in Hawaii. Here, however, Mr. Smith was pretty sure Keeler broke into the safe because he fled northern California and due to the "circumstances." Due to Hawaii's long distance away from the California gold region, there was little hope that Mr. Smith would ever recover the lost four thousand dollars.
[323] *Ibid.,* p. 262.

To day the Doct' came up from Roses Bar to see Mr Sommers had to open his foot in a new place I think his case may yet be doubtful he suffers largely from it Therm 63 morn 96 shade 110 sun 78 eve.[324]

During the last two days of July, Kingsley finished working on some "machines." Other miners he knew installed timbers, which made a kind of bridge across the American River. Kingsley also continued working on "rifflers" to four more "machines." On Saturday, August 2, "Mr Ayers started for Sac [Sacramento] City to get canvass for the dam."[325]

Kingsley continued his work on the quicksilver "boxes." Monday, August 12, was a special day for Kingsley because he

went to setting up the riddles to day[.] The canvass came in to night —Mr Ayers brought me four letters three from New Preston & one from Illinois they were daded [dated] They afforded a rich feast especially here in this country and must say that I hardly know how to reward the kindness of thier [their] authors.

On August 14, Kingsley and Smith realized that the incorporation of their company, the New Haven & California Joint Stock Company, had taken place fourteen months ago. It was clear that "we could not raise money enough to take ourselves all home so that it is bad for the ones who fitted out its members."[326]

They might have been discouraged at this point, but they persisted in building their dam.

[324] *Ibid.,* p. 366.

[325] *Ibid.,* p. 367.

[326] *Ibid.,* p. 370. This comment by Kingsley showed that he understood the individual toll on the families and investors back home who had freely invested their money on the Connecticut company. It was clear to him and probably to every one of his coworkers that they were not going to be able to recoup even the funds that many had put out to get their enterprise started back in the spring of 1849.

On Tuesday, August 1 I worked at getting the machines finished a job that I hope this week to accomplish Received a fine letter from Miss W a great treat and must give a full answer.[327]

On Thursday, August 22, he wrote,

Worked at the Panning troughs got out the stuff & put the bottoms in the water to swell them bfore putting them together, it requires great care in making both these and the riffler boxes in order to have them hold quicksilver[.] Therm 63 morn 102 shade 120 sun 83 eve Sent down a letter to Marysville to be mailed to Miss W.[328]

For some, the unrelenting heat may have been the straw that broke the camel's back. The oppressive heat and their persistent frustration over the low yield in gold sapped the determination of some who had been trying to stick it out at the same location. On Saturday, August 24, he wrote,

The Co [company] did not work in the afternoon as some refused on account of haveing [having] to "slim a team" but I think at this time every hours labor ought to count 'till we get into the river, Mr Wm Foster & myself took our pans and went up the river about two miles prospecting we tumbled down some rocks and get a little dirt from the crevasses and panned out some 4 or 5 dollars worth in a short time, the country up through this is extremely wild & romantic the river is hemmed in on both sides with huge masses of rocks and making to these on the right hand side is the steep mountain which is rocky & precipitous in places with some tall straight pines shooting up towards heaven as if unconscious of the steeps below & above them, on the left the huge rocks rise perpendicular overhanging in some places & jutting out as if ready to tumble from their places into the

[327] *Ibid.,* p. 371.
[328] *Ibid.,* p. 371.

stream below, these rise to the hight [height] of several hundred feet from the surface of the water presenting a black frightful appearance in going along beneath them the water of the river along beneath them the water of the river along here is set back by our dam and runs silently as if affraid [afraid] to disturb the tomblike silence of the place the water is verry [very] deep along here, and the rocks near the water are worn high up smooth by the freshets that take place here in the spring.[329]

Only someone with such a deeply spiritual soul as Nelson Kingsley had could write such a description of northern California's rugged natural wonder and beauty. Today, one doesn't have to go far to experience something of that same wonder at Nature's beauty.

The daily intense heat continued throughout August. On August 29, he wrote,

We have gotten into a place of more substantial stuff to fill in with being more turf received a New York Herald of July 13th which *contained* the death of the President Taylor. This news was truely [truly] sudden to us all and at this crisis in congress when the slave question-and other matters of so much importance are to be finished or decided I was truly in hopes we could have had his wise old head in determining and adjusting them to the best interests of our great nation but it seems we have a man that bids fair to be a man to take his place.[330]

In light of this profoundly disturbing national news, it was hard to keep working away at their dam. On top of all that was happening back east, rumors of big strikes supposedly close filled Kingsley's ears. At the end of August, there was a story that at a place called Segars Bar, nine miles below them on the river, the miners were taking out "from 20 to 60 pounds pr [per] day."[331] On

---

[329] *Ibid.,* p. 372.

[330] *Ibid.,* p. 373.

[331] *Ibid.,* p. 374.

September 4, "news came up today that 501 dollars was taken out of the bed of the river at Roses Bar about 4 miles below here."[332]

Kingsley was now a member of a party of four that had worked at the same general location on the American River for four months since May. There had been a new rumor of fabulous riches nearly every week since then, but true or not, they knew that even if it took working more weeks where they were, they at least had some chance of coming away a little bit better off. Giving up their claim would net them nothing, so they kept at it.

During the first week of October, they found a few unmistakable signs of gold. On October 8, Kingsley wrote, "Did not quite finish clearing off today, find a plenty of "Oro" sticking to the stones as we came down to the good dirt.[333] On October 9, they were finally making a little at Union Bar: "Worked at washing in the afternoon washed 25 barrow loads and got 5 oz 15 pwts or 92 dolls [dollars] of amalgam we panned out of small iron pan $4.75 cts [cents] this afternoon in picked dirt."[334] The next day, Kingsley thought each man's earnings would be about fifty dollars. He wryly noted, "This is good but not big for this country this is $284.80 cts [cents]."[335] On Friday, October 11, he remarked that on that day, they "did not go through so much dirt as yesterday," with their take being $239.60.

At last, they were getting results. He ventured an opinion.

> The rest are doing well on the bar and I believe all will get well paid who are engaged in getting gold here. Things bear a little different appearance now to what they did two months ago as the bar has more than trebled its population in that time.[336]

Societal customs differed in California compared to home in Connecticut. Working on Sunday wasn't considered as "Sabbath breaking" as it was in New England. On October 19, he noted their earnings in the last week were "1,296

---

[332] *Ibid.*, p. 374.
[333] *Ibid.*, p. 384.
[334] *Ibid.*, p. 384.
[335] *Ibid.*, p. 384.
[336] *Ibid.*, p. 384.

dollars."[337] This was certainly a welcome change for him and his long-suffering coworkers.

On October 20, he left camp with Harry Smith to buy nine hundred dollars' worth of supplies to carry them through the winter. The path to Sacramento took them to Ousleys Bridge on the Bear River. Kingsley remarked they slept "with a full accompaniment of flees [fleas] to comfort us during the night." After crossing the flat land northeast of Sacramento, they "forded the American River about 2 miles from its mouth and to the city about four oclock [o'clock]."[338]

On October 24, two days after reaching Sacramento, Kingsley suffered a bout of severe diarrhea (or "cholera morbus"), probably from drinking polluted water.

> I went to the vessel and they tried to have me take the lobelia but I thought nature had done her duty in the line of purging and concluded not to try it and was well in the afternoon[.] Our teamsters arrived last night that are to haul our goods.[339]

Despite his limited success in gold mining, Kingsley was plagued by thoughts of giving up and returning home. He realized that he would have to wait and continue working because he still didn't have enough gold to pay for a return trip and take something home with him for his bride. They dug a twelve-feet-deep hole beside the river, yet the results were meager. He commented, "It is slow getting dirt ours to day gave us 4 oz 16 pwt 6 grs." He was stressed out and weak. He was "very sore across my bowels, am taking Mrs Kidders Cordial so much recommended by some but I think dieting to be the best remedy unless the disease is too severe."[340]

On November 17, Kingsley doubted that Long Bar had much more potential left in it for gain. Two days later, it rained almost all day. On Sunday, November 24, he

---

[337] *Ibid.,* p. 384.

[338] *Ibid.,* p. 386. There were no such things as insect repellent or window screens.

[339] *Ibid.,* p. 387.

[340] *Ibid.,* p. 390.

went up to Boston Bar-which place is now entirely deserted rambled about awhile with Mr. John Grew and Lewis Swift no rain to day. Brisco came in with a fine deer at night.[341]

The location change gradually paid off, yet their gain wasn't nearly as much as they'd hoped for. The next day, the weather was clear. They worked on Boston Bar and "got 2 oz 5 pwts or 36 dolls [dollars] amalgam have not got down low enough to have it good."[342] While Kingsley bemoaned their paltry gains, on the next Tuesday another friend, Edwin Ayer, came back from Sacramento with the good news that the cholera sickness there had subsided a little. They still had four at work. November 27, another workday, yielded them $58.26. Kingsley had trouble containing his frustration. The last three days of November were too rainy to work. On November 30, Kingsley wrote,

> This morning the ravine is full of water tumbling down by, and the river has so swollen during the day that it is about 4 feet higher that at its lowest stage this season, completely inundating all the claims so that it renders working to gain anything about out of the question, the river to day is running with such force over the falls below the dam that it is continually moveing [moving] rocks in the bed of the stream making a considerable noise & rumbling.[343]

With a typically cold and rainy northern California winter underway, Kingsley was happy to turn to one of his normal pastimes: singing with others on Sundays. Another friend, Mr. Coleman, "got smart enough to go home,"[344] leaving the American River claims for Falmouth, Massachusetts on December 1.

Although Kingsley wasn't exactly getting rich, the first week of December saw his party netting, on separate days, $24, $110, $138, and $65 during the first week of December. Not far away, Mr. Wright's party was taking out more.

---

[341] *Ibid.,* p. 392.

[342] *Ibid.,* p. 392.

[343] *Ibid.,* p. 393.

[344] *Ibid.,* p. 393. Coleman was the first miner to decide to return home. More would soon follow.

On December 11, he was disappointed in only getting "2 oz 3-18 which does not pay us wages."[345] They didn't give up. On Thursday, December 12, their work resulted in "twenty-seven dollars' worth of gold amalgam."[346] Results of their mining on December 13 were encouraging. Their Boston Bar claim netted them more than nine ounces of gold in the morning alone. Perseverance was yielding steady yet small results.

Others had somewhat better results working the claim next to theirs. "One of their hands to[ok] a common pan the size of a large milk pan and got 121/2 dollars." Kingsley took off Sunday, December 15. Kingsley wrote, "Drawed and wrote a little to send to Marble Dale."[347]

Northern California's winter weather made its mark on the mining community. Early Monday morning, December 16, there was a storm. Kingsley noted,

> A bad night last night about 1 oclock a gale passed over us which threatned [threatened] to blow the trees up by the roots, and tear every tent into ribbands [ribbons] it blew down several flat but mine stood it finely, give me a good log house in a gale, but a tent will do verry [very] well at any other time. The Dutchman's large tent blew down with his wife and several others sleeping in it at the time which was rather hard for her but she is a woman of strong constitution and will stand as much as most of us.[348]

As Kingsley had often done when at sea, he noted unusual weather in his diary.

This was remarkable for him to note something that happened to someone other than members of his own company. This was one of few times that a woman was mentioned in Kingsley's account. Work continued to clear off dirt

---

[345] *Ibid.*, p. 394.

[346] *Ibid.*, p. 395.

[347] *Ibid.*, p. 394.

[348] *Ibid.*, p. 395.

and debris from their claim. On December 19, he observed how the gold vein diminished the closer they got to the river.

> They have not been doing as well to day in the hole joining [[adjoining] us as they are too near the river which has been proved [proven] more than once as it seems to fail in all cases that when we get so far towards the river the vein of dirt that is the richest runs out.[349]

---

349 *Ibid.*, p. 395.

Nelson Kingsley sees the Elephant
The sketch above and all previous sketches are used by
permission of The Society of California Pioneers

CHAPTER 9

Nelson Kingsley Sees the Elephant

Without him even being aware of it, Kingsley's homesickness had become stronger than his gold fever. He yearned to be back home and in the arms of his sweetheart and fiancée. On the night before his second Christmas in northern California, he recalled precious Christmases at home. Obviously he sorely missed New England.

> To night being so pleasant, and the night before Christmas I almost wish myself among my friends at home I can however imagine how they are doing. The choirs are chanting hymns of praise. Many an able sermon is written to enlighten the minds of the people, and all is bustle & confusion, sleigh bells perhaps are pealing forth their merry tones, to many joyous hearts, but here I am away from all these lovely scenes toiling away, for what, that which may yet afford me comfort at some future day. Still I but little know what use many be made of it. Therefore I will spend as little time here as possible.[350]

Christmas in 1850 on the American River in northern California's mining region was not like any Nelson Kingsley had known before in Connecticut. As he noted on Christmas Day 1850, he worked, instead of relaxing and enjoying a good time.

> A beautiful day.... I hardly think they have had a more pleasant day in New England. I worked on the bar at clearing off today and have now got so that tomorrow we shall wash My luxuries to day are limited as far as eatables is [are] concerned for breakfast

---

[350] *Ibid.*, p. 397.

fried ham-doughnuts & crackers & cheese &c for dinner about the same, and for supper stewed Oysters which were fresh & nice they come from Boston, in sealed tins and taste as fresh and delicious as they would have done the day they were put up.[351]

December 26 seemed to be a bit more productive than any they'd had before in December. They came away with "13 ounces 11 dollars in amalgam[.] George Brisco worked with us."[352] They did even slightly better on the December 27 and got "14 ounces 7 dollars in amalgam."[353]

They were about to make up their minds on whether to keep working and stay where they were, or to quit and move on somewhere else. On Saturday, December 28, he noted,

> Clear, not a cloud to be seen and as warm as summer. Worked at washing did not get as much to-day only got 9 ounces 13 dollars in amalgam. We shall [see] if it holds clear find out whether our claim will be as rich as the others have been along side of us next week.[354]

Kingsley kept abreast of what success other miners at work on the bar near him were having. On December 29, he only cut a little wood. Two days later, on Tuesday, December 31, they "got 8 oz 14 dolls [dollars] Therm 34 – 64 – 44 Old Year Out."[355]

With the start of 1851, their washing produced significantly better results; at least early in January. On New Year's Day, they "got 29 ounces & 15 dollars amalgam which is verry [very] near a hundred dollars a piece [apiece] in clear gold[.]"[356] On Thursday, January 2, "We worked at washing and done a better

---

[351] *Ibid.*, p. 397.

[352] *Ibid.*, p. 397.

[353] If Kingsley's 14 ounces had been pure gold, he would have been paid $224.00 at the Mint.

[354] *Ibid.*, p. 398.

[355] *Ibid.*, p. 398.

[356] *Ibid.*, p. 398.

days work than we did yesterday, we got 41 ounces & 15 dollars in amalgam."[357] Adding up their gains for the past two weeks, they totaled twelve hundred dollars in gold earnings. On January 7, their proceeds for three hours of work were "4 ounces & 4 dollars in amalgam this afternoon."[358]

Although Kingsley could take credit in knowing his efforts at mining at last were somewhat successful, sadly the new year also brought with it more sickness and weakness from diarrhea. On January 16 and 17, he wrote,

> Clear to day but a little cooler. Worked in the forenoon but lay off in the afternoon with a headache I do not like this strain of ailing that has prowled about me the past week, but as my diarrhea has left me I hope soon to be myself again as I find comfort in idleness.

> Friday, 17th. The day has been a fine one. I worked to day with the rest feeling considerable [considerably] better, we washed to-day most of the time and got 10 ounces & 5 dollars.[359]

Water began filling the hole they had just dug. On January 18, they removed a total of ten ounces and twelve dollars of gold. On Sunday, January 20, Kingsley noted,

> Some packers came in to day with a few goods to sell Potatoes are down to 18 cts [cents] pr lb which shows quite a difference between now and the price last season then they were sold below here for three dollars a pound ... packers brought rumor of an even greater strike than the "Gold Lake" excitement.[360]

Ever since his company's arrival in the mining district two years earlier, as we have seen, they had heard rumors of fantastic new strikes being discovered

---

[357] *Ibid.,* p. 400.

[358] *Ibid.,* p. 401.

[359] *Ibid.,* p. 402.

[360] *Ibid.,* p. 402. By 1851, California's farmers were producing bigger crop yields, which brought some prices down a little.

elsewhere. By early 1851, Kingsley was accustomed to hearing such tall tales. Especially with their recent moderate success, he took this new rumor with a greater grain of salt. He and his coworkers were not about to give up on their claim even if they had less success than some.

On January 20, they began using a pump to remove water from their hole. They also had some success with "the machine running on the top dirt in the last clearing and got 13 ounces 11 dollars in amalgam."[361] Their work party rose in number to seven. They continued getting a bit more than ten ounces per day until Friday, January 24. His mind returned to the idea of leaving.

> A fine day & a cool night last night but not so as to be at all uncomfortably so. I cannot find aught against such weather as this and it not only is as good as we can wish to work in but it allows me to cherish the idea that we can work our claims out before spring opens, or high water drives us out and if this is accomplished I think I shall vamose[.] We worked washing the top streak to day & clearing out red sand we got 14 oz & 9 dollars.[362]

In his next entry, January 25, Kingsley stated, "Retorted to night and had 1256 dollars which we divided after paying $180 expenses."[363] If their party was seven individuals, each one was entitled to about $153.[364]

On Sunday, January 26, he and a coworker took a break to go on a long hike for a change of scene. After reaching a crossroads with frame buildings, built by settlers, the pair visited an Indian village.

> I took a walk of eight miles to day over the hills to Roses Bar with Mr Blakeslee we went down across Deer Creek and found a number of frame buildings ... it is a general crossing place

---

[361] *Ibid.*, p. 402.

[362] *Ibid.*, p. 403.

[363] *Ibid.*, p. 403.

[364] *Ibid.*, p. 403. In today's currency this amount of gold would be three thousand eighty dollars apiece.

I believe to the mines on the south & Middle Forks of the
Yuba. A little farther on we stopped at an Indian rancheria
and amused ourselves with looking about them as they were
verry Friendly, but the general style of the buildings I think
presents as striking a contrast to our mode of living in tents
as tents do to the best architecture the wigwams are made of
sticks and weeds about four feet high with a hole in the top to
let the smoke out The entrance is a little hole big enough to
crawl in on ones hands & knees-the women are filthy looking
and go naked save a few rags about the loins, the children are
entirely naked—the men-boys and some of the young squaws
have on some clothes, but these they hardly know how to
put on the same as they should be, some will have on an old
shirt and nothing els [else]—some a verry good coat or a pair
of pants—and some as many old rags and clothes as they can
make hang about them, on the whole I think these digger
Indians are the lowest, most ignorant and degraded of any
race of being I ever read of.[365]

Kingsley returned by way of Roses Bar, noting "there does not seem to be
much going on."[366] It was "a little after dark and refreshed myself with a slice
of Cold Ham some bread & butter and Hot tea-which my worthy partner Mr
Bennett had taken pains to keep nice & warm for me."[367]

Kingsley and his coworkers were working a second hole but were getting
less gold than earlier at their previous claim. On January 28, they got just "7
ounces & 9 dollars."[368] He confessed to thinking about selling his claim, "I would

---

[365] *Ibid.*, pp. 403–404. Kingsley's description of an Indian rancheria is like others from the gold
rush era. Whatever some of us today may think about it, he wasn't writing for us, a modern
audience. It was his own description written in a diary, meant only for his family or possibly
some friends. Unlike Delavan and Delano, who had been professional writers before they'd
journeyed to California, Kingsley's diary is clearly a reliable account.

[366] *Ibid.*, p. 404.

[367] *Ibid.*, p. 404.

[368] *Ibid.*, p. 404.

sell cheap tonight or for 500 dollars but yet I think it cannot fail."[369] However, before another month had passed, he would sell his claim for much less.

Kingsley wasn't the only forty-niner thinking of selling a claim. On the following day, Wednesday, January 29, as they dug out just

> 6 oz & 4 dollars which is rather small pay to what we anticipated last week and judgeing from the way our other hole paid us. Mr Platt sold out his share to day, to Messrs Whipple and Blackman. He got 500 dollars for his share which takeing [taking] the show as we now have it I think was a plenty I think I would sell for that tonight if any one felt disposed to take the offer but as I am not over anxious to start for home just yet I will hold on awhile longer.[370]

Kingsley recorded that "Mr. Platt" was selling out and returning his home in Mobile, Alabama. Platt did very well. In his next entry, Kingsley said he was at least somewhat envious of the southerner. As noted earlier, Mr. Whipple was the second director, next in the line of command to Mr. Smith. On the next day, Kingsley pursued his own curiosity by taking the day off to look over Mr. Platt's former claim.

> I went down to Longs Bar to pack some things for Platt who takes the stage from Marysvill [Marysville]-he has left with about 1700 dollars, and will soon be with his family in Mobile. The boys have been clearing off some that was left of the red sand, and washed some, and got 5 oz 14 dolls [dollars].[371]

Because it was raining heavily, the miners stopped work. Rainy weather and snow are normal this time of year in northern California. On January 31, they mined ten ounces, and on February 1, their gain was over twenty-five ounces. On Sunday, February 2, Kingsley, "reported the last four days work

---

[369] *Ibid.*, p. 405.

[370] *Ibid.*, p. 405.

[371] *Ibid.*, p. 405.

and after paying expenses for help divided 125 dollars this fell a little short of 12 dollars pr ounce had a fine sing in the evening with three or four other hombres."[372]

It was a hard fact that when the forty-niners exchanged their gold for currency, most placer miners had to settle for less than sixteen dollars an ounce for the results of their hard-earned labor. This reality was also shown by more forty-niner diaries in previous chapters.

Although Nelson Kingsley had been in California for about a year and half, California slang (even some Spanish words) had become part of his speech. Despite managing to get thirty-five ounces and four dollars in gold on February 3, Kingsley fretted that the better weather soon might end. There were five in Kingsley's work crew. They only had a thirty-five-foot long stretch to clear and work. On February 5, they got nine ounces and thirteen dollars, and on the following day, they got nine more ounces and four dollars. On Friday, February 7, Kingsley put up his claim for sale for three hundred dollars. He had to continue working because at first it did not sell.

Kingsley had begun using a few more common Spanish words like Sabado (Saturday) and Domingo (Sunday). On Domingo, February 8, they retorted their ore. As a result, they got $816 worth of gold. Kingsley stated, "It seems now as if the time could not slip away too fast till the middle of next month[,] March, the time set for going home."[373] It is probable that Kingsley and at least some of the other company members had decided to sell out and leave in March 1851, two years after they had sailed from New Haven. Because Mr. Platt had recently sold his claim and left, Kingsley decided to follow suit sooner than planned. At this time, Kingsley's party numbered five.

An unusual thing happened on February 12. While they took out three ounces and eleven dollars, Kingsley was glad he was not as bad off as some others were,

> To day men have come along 'dead broke' and have to work for
> 4 dollars pr [per] day to get enough to take them to some other
> place when I see so many roveing [roving] about the country

---

[372] *Ibid.,* pp. 405–406.

[373] Ibid., p. 407.

without a cent as it were, trying to find it but cant [can't.] I think I am a lucky chap and had not better stop to spend what I have got trying to get more, at times I feel sorry and a little disappointed to thing [think] I have laid up no more but I cannot blame myself and must try to do the best I can on a little.[374]

In the next two days, February 13 and 14, they got a total of "seventeen ounces and nine dollars' worth of gold. This will just about pay us wages from the time we commenced clearing off." On Tuesday, February 18, Kingsley noted, "I sold my claim to day for two hundred dollars to Mr Samuel O Whitmore."[375]

On the next day, his coworkers also sold. They began making preparations to return home. On Friday, February 21, Kingsley and Messrs Whipple, Brisco, and Blackman began their trip southwestward on the steamer back to San Francisco. Kingsley noted,

> Theodore Turner packed our things down to Longs Bar where we took the stage to Marysville[.] We got to the city about 4 oclock [o'clock] and put up at the Southern & Western Hotel ... as my sight was small to induce me to stop longer I thought now to be as good a time as any to leave.... A number of new and substantial buildings have gone up since I was here in July last. The plains between here and long bar are in spots fenced in and some beautiful farms are now going forward.[376]

He was optimistic about the future for these farms if rainfall was sufficient. Kingsley also mentioned that he promised several of his friends that when he returned home, he would write to them about the current price of gold and what his voyage back to Connecticut had cost.

On Saturday, February 22, they boarded the steamer *Lawrence*, each paying the five-dollar fare. They arrived in Sacramento at 9:00 p.m. On the next day, Sunday, February 23, he walked around Sacramento. There were some

---

[374] *Ibid.*, p. 407.
[375] *Ibid.*, p. 408.
[376] *Ibid.*, p. 408.

new gambling houses, and he was impressed by their talented musicians. On
Sunday, February 23, Kingsley wrote,

> I went aboard the bark which lies in the American stream, and
> found a few of the old company on board who are in the fishing
> business[.] I arraigned [arranged] what little I possessed aboard
> & left for San Francisco in the steamer *Hartford* The fare is down
> to one dollar and will not soon be up again to its old rates as
> there seems to plenty of first rate steam boats for conveyance
> of passengers on the rivers in this country.[377]

It was rainy in San Francisco on Monday, February 24, when they arrived.
When he awoke, Kingsley found himself on board the steamboat already tied up
at Long Wharf. He went ashore to obtain passage on a ship bound for Panama.
The town seemed to him teeming with "a great number of people," and the
mail steamer *Columbus* had just "anchored off Rincoln [Rincon] Point."[378] Rents
for building space were high, from six hundred to eight hundred dollars a
month. A man named Stuart was rumored to have murdered someone.

> The citizens were for takeing [taking] him out of the station
> house and hanging him but the long rigmarole of law finally
> prevailed and quiet restored. The city is full of rascals and men
> who are doing business will not stand and be trod on by such
> Murderous Villainous rascals as are at present prowling about
> the city, the only way is to make an example of all thieves.[379]

Kingsley and other members of his company, who were bound for Panama
to start their trip home, had a decision to make: pay more for passage aboard
one of a number of steamers, or pay less to travel on a sailing ship, which would
take longer. The difference in price was considerable. One hundred twenty-five
dollars for a steamer passage versus fifty dollars for the sailing ship. They chose

---

[377] *Ibid.,* p. 410.

[378] *Ibid.,* p. 410.

[379] *Ibid.,* p. 410.

to pay fifty dollars to take the slower vessel. Kingsley was satisfied, knowing he'd saved seventy-five dollars. The name of the brig he chose was *Annah*. He decided to turn down at least two offers of speculators who asked him to go into business with them if he'd be willing to commit all the pile he'd earned mining gold. He decided not to take on any new business in which he had no experience and which might be risky.

While in San Francisco on Friday, February 28, Kingsley began by looking at fruit for sale

> at the fruit store of Norton & Pearl oranges sell for 25 to 371/2 [cents?] apiece, and lemons bring any price[.] Limes Bananas, and a few poor apples are in the market and sell for large prices, as it is verry [very] difficult to get fruit here as nice as we do in the Eastern states.[380]

Kingsley couldn't resist checking out the gambling halls. As he had been in Sacramento, he was impressed by progress in construction in San Francisco. He noted that there were impressive new buildings being built.

> Most of them are gambling houses of fashionable resort and in some of them some three or four s good musicians are playing as I ever heard in any place which is calculated to draw crouds [crowds] into the spacious saloons, where every inducement is held out to try our luck at most all kinds of games but it is hard to beat any man at his own game so I never thought it best to even try to win.[381]

While awaiting their date to get underway, Kingsley witnessed the excitement surrounding two fires, which broke out on two successive days and came close to the *Annah*. The first fire broke out on the steamer *Santa Clara* tied up on Long Wharf, which also damaged the *Hartford*, the same steamer he'd been on from Sacramento to San Francisco. The second fire happened to be far

---

[380] *Ibid.,* p. 411.
[381] *Ibid.,* p. 412.

enough away from their vessel as to be no threat although several buildings burned down.

On March 4, 1851, he wrote the last entry in his diary.

> We droped [dropped] down a little this morning and anchored, to let the captain go ashore to get his clearance, lots of grumbling is going on among the passengers ... We raised our anchor about 4 P M and droped [dropped] down around Clarks Point to be ready to go to sea to morrow, things generally in a peaceable condition to night.[382]

Kingsley noted that many of his fellow passengers hadn't been aboard a sailing ship like this one before. This accounted for their naiveté about such a voyage would be like. On March 5, 1851, as the *Annah* sailed out of the Golden Gate and into the sea, perhaps Kingsley chuckled a little to himself and even shook his head as he recalled the toll his long voyage to California during 1849 had taken on him and the other New Haven and California Joint Stock Company members.

* * *

According to Mr. Kingsley's editor, Professor Teggert, in the latter half of 1851, after his explorations and placer mining efforts were all completed and upon returning to Connecticut, Kingsley married his betrothed lady. Miss E. W. became Mrs. Nelson W. Kingsley. Sadly, however, they had no children, and Kingsley died in 1852. Probably his overall health had suffered greatly from pursuing his dream in the northern California mines, particularly the numerous severe episodes of cholera. It is also quite possible that, like many others who had to brave the dangerous trip across tropical Panama, he may have contracted a disease like yellow fever or malaria. He could have been snakebit, bitten by a monkey or another animal, or even shot by someone he'd encountered there.

In 1851, after his return home, Nelson gave his diary to his sister, Mrs. John Hungerford. When she died, her daughter, Mrs. Nellie Fairchild, took over its

---

[382] *Ibid.*, p. 413.

possession. In 1888, she gave it to Nathan Kingsley, who was Nelson's nephew. In 1910, Nathan presented it for safe keeping to the University of California's Bancroft Library.

In 1914, Frederick J. Teggart, associate professor of Pacific Coast History at the University of California at Berkeley, California, and curator of the Academy of Pacific Coast History, edited and published Nelson Kingsley's diary. It is a copy of this version that I have taken excerpts from here. In the introduction to this book, Professor Teggart wrote,

> The diary is written on two hundred and seven pages of a two hundred and twenty-four page blank book, 8 × 10 1/2 inches in size. The fly-leaves at the back contain sketches of places touched at on the voyage; among them are Port au Grande, Cape Verde Islands, and Port Stanley, Falkland Islands.
>
> In printing, the punctuation and spelling of the original have been scrupulously followed; lack of punctuation is indicated by spaces. The characters < > indicates matter printed in proper, but not in original order—such as marginal additions.[383]

Kingsley was a sensitive, intelligent, multitalented, and devout Christian gentleman whose record as a miner mirrored many other forty-niners. He didn't strike it as rich as he'd originally hoped to do as a result of becoming an argonaut. Also, like so many others, his travel and extremely strenuous, dangerous work in the diggings eventually led to his premature death. Unlike many other miners, though, he remained physically, spiritually, and mentally true to his family and to his fiancée, Miss E. W. His diary is the most well-written and poignant of the others that make up the chapters in this book.

---

[383] *Diary of Nelson Kingsley, a California Argonaut, of 1849*, ed. Frederick J. Teggart (Berkeley, CA: University of California Press, 1914), p. 237.

CHAPTER 10

Robert Stedman, Marin County Builder

Looking back at those who acted on their golden dreams from today's perspective, some tend to group all the miners together as if somehow they fit in one tidy, miniscule mold. Nothing could have been further from the truth. We have seen a diverse group of individuals, each of whom was greatly different from the others.

Before Robert was born, the Stedman family lived in Rhode Island and Massachusetts. Robert's parents, Oliver and Elizabeth Stedman, had a large family. Robert was born on February 6, 1809.[384] He had two brothers and nine sisters; three of his siblings died in infancy. Robert was six feet tall and was an avid outdoorsman with a genial, easygoing disposition, which helped him fit into almost any group.

His first job was as an apprentice paper maker in one of the paper mills in Berkshire County. Changing course while still young, he first became a millwright. Then he became a carpenter. He was rated as an expert carpenter before he left New England late in 1848 to travel to California.

After arriving in San Francisco, like nearly every other forty-niner argonaut, Robert traveled to today's El Dorado County late in 1849. He had excellent results, and after succeeding in gold mining in 1850, he returned home to the East Coast. He invested his gold in land and built a hotel in Lenox, Massachusetts. He left his wife in charge of the hotel and an attached grocery store, which he also built. In 1853 Robert returned to northern California. He resettled there, thus succeeding in business on both ends of North America.

When he had reached the age of twenty-four, Robert married a young

---

[384] See Bertha Stedman Rothwell, *Biographical Sketch of Robert Stedman*, unpublished manuscript, p. 1, on loan to the author by Steve Stedman, February, 2019.

woman, Elvira Dorman. The ceremony took place in Otis, Massachusetts, on January 29, 1843. Three of her ancestors had signed the Mayflower Compact in 1620. The couple started a family. They had four sons, including Robert, all of whom went to California at least for a short time. They also had a daughter. Robert worked as a builder "in and about Lenox, Massachusetts."[385] Besides his construction work, Robert also owned and operated a small teamster company that consisted of three large freight wagons. Workdays began early because the wagons were used to transport charcoal, which had to be delivered to the Lenox Glass furnace. Their sons, Lawrence (age eleven) and Robert Jr. (age ten), had to be ready each day to leave the house at 2:00 a.m. to drive the horse-drawn wagons. The glass factory had to fire up its glass furnaces early each day to meet its production output goals. With their father driving the lead wagon, the boys would doze off. Their horses would simply follow the lead horse.

When the unusual and amazing news arrived throughout the East Coast that gold was discovered in California, Oliver Stedman and Robert Stedman started making plans to take on the risk of making the journey to San Francisco. Oliver, who was Robert's younger brother, picked up the nickname Commy. His cousin was Commodore Oliver Hazard Perry, commander of the American vessels that had defeated the British during the War of 1812 on Lake Erie.

Returning to the Stedman brothers, they each decided to leave their families behind in Massachusetts.[386] They went by ship around Cape Horn. The ship made excellent time because it rounded Cape Horn and docked in San Francisco on March 21, 1849. The Stedman brothers wasted little time seeing San Francisco or Sacramento. As soon as possible, they equipped themselves with a tent and mining tools. They began prospecting in El Dorado County. They were able to remove a sizable amount of gold. As soon as they could, they made the return trip by sea to Massachusetts in 1850.

Robert was especially fortunate in that his "poke" was large enough that he

---

[385] The author is endebted to his friend and fellow member and former president of the Western Sonoma County Historical Society, Sebastopol, California for the use of his family's record recorded as noted above by Ms. Bertha Stedman.

[386] At the end of 1848, they sailed from New York City aboard the *Samoset*. Samoset was the Indian name of the Native American who first greeted the pilgrims aboard the English ship, "Mayflower." His name means "One who travels much."

reinvested most of it to buy a lot in a newly developing part of his hometown of Lenox. The lot was a prominent corner lot in a residential area of town. He employed his building talents to construct a two-story hotel that his wife and family operated for many profitable years. In fact, when his descendant, Bertha Stedman Rothwell, paid a visit there about a hundred years later, the structure still stood, none the worse for wear.[387] The new section of Lenox was named Lenox Dale. Robert included a grocery store. He named his hotel the El Dorado Hotel. He built it as a room and board facility for Lenox Glass Factory employees.

Robert had had such success in California earlier that he made up his mind to leave his wife a second time to make another journey west. Elvira became the hotel manager while Robert's daughter and son-in-law, Mr. and Mrs. Leroy Kellogg, managed the grocery business. Robert brought with him his fifteen-year-old son, Stephen Schuler Stedman, sailing to the east coast of Panama.

Once they reached San Francisco, they set out for the American River. They hadn't been working long there when news came of a whole new gold discovery on the Fraser River in British Columbia. Stephen was taken with a new golden dream, and he left California to head north to British Columbia. He worked there for the next twelve years while his father went back to San Francisco. Robert was forty-five in 1854, with the gold rush essentially over. He noticed that supplies of lumber were very short in San Francisco, so Robert paid special attention to the large redwood and Douglas fir forests in Marin County. Changing career courses once more, he moved to the tiny hamlet of Lagunitas, a few miles northwest of San Rafael, where he resumed his trade as a lumberman and builder. There were groves of redwoods close by. Using the wood from a gigantic redwood he felled, he built himself a small house during the fall of 1854. California had no sawmills, so woodsmen had only hand tools such as double-headed axes, cross-cut saws, and wedges to cut down trees. Once logs were brought back to lumbermen's workrooms, they could be cut into lumber with "files, a saw-set, a grind stone, and whet-stone."[388]

It was not too long before the demand for both lumber and the construction of barns and farmhouses became more than one man could handle. Robert hired

---

[387] Family genealogist Mrs. Bertha S. Rothwell toured the hotel in 1947.

[388] Ibid., p. 10.

other men to work in both fields. One essential tool Stedman did not have was a froe. To get one, he had to ride to San Rafael to a blacksmith. A few days later, he returned and picked up the tool, to which he later attached a sturdy handle made out of laurel wood. He needed the froe to make shingles. He prepared bundles of shingles. Each shingle had to be six inches wide by sixteen inches long. He also produced shakes for the roofs of dairy barns; each shake had to be three feet long by seven inches wide. The shingles and shakes were a uniform three-eighths of an inch in thickness. In 1865 Robert provided the materials and supervised the construction of twenty buildings of the Pacific Powder Mill Company, located on Daniels Creek, a mile and half north of Lagunitas.

After the fact, he learned of the passing of his wife, Elvira, from one of their daughters who lived near her mother back East. Elvira died on January 21, 1858. After learning this bad news, Robert decided to give up the idea of returning back to Lenox. Like many who followed him in his own generation and in generations to come, he had fallen completely in love with the beautiful, majestic groves of redwood trees of Marin County and elsewhere, just inland from the Pacific Coast.

Some six years after Elvira's death, Robert almost had to mourn the death of his son, Robert S. Stedman. The young man had gone up the British Columbia to work in the fur trade. It was either in 1867 or 1868 that he was badly wounded in a fight with some Canadian Indians. He returned from a hospital in Victoria, British Canada, with the help of a male nurse. He was weak and weighed less than one hundred pounds, and his father believed he would die. However, according to Mrs. Rothwell's account, Robert Sr. found a beehive in a hollow of a redwood tree that contained a good supply of honey. The taste of this honey was so captivating that the wounded man began to eat again, and soon his wounds healed. Father and son worked together for several years after the son's return to health.

When the Transcontinental Railroad was completed in 1869, Stephen Stedman went back to Lenox aboard the first train. After the train arrived in Massachusetts, Stephen and Miss Lucy Jane Hall of Monterey were married. After a short visit, the young married couple and his younger brother, Byron (nineteen at the time), returned to California in October 1869. The father and son continued to work as loggers, lumbermen, and builders. Byron, on the other hand, tried his hand at various jobs, including driving a sixteen-horse team pulling a harvester, but he eventually returned to Lee, Massachusetts. His fare on the transcontinental railroad was just $129. Byron later became a successful dentist in New York.

The two Stedmans continued working as lumbermen in Lagunitas. They also filled orders for pickets and posts for the dairies of Marin and southern Sonoma County. By the 1870s, sawmills were replacing hand-hewn lumber. For example, in 1874 Isaac Shaver set up "a portable saw-mill of [on] the White Ranch about one mile south of San Geronimo Station."[389] Shaver joined forces with Edmund and Samuel Kiler to set up another sawmill in 1875, which had a daily output of twelve hundred board feet of lumber. Mrs. Rothwell's mother, Lucy Hall Stedman, made notes that included one about a redwood tree nine feet in diameter felled by the three Stedmans. It yielded one hundred thousand shingles as well as a great deal of cordwood. Its bark, which measured "eight to ten inches in thickness,"[390] went into planking for wagon bridge, which was used for many years instead of more permanent steel bars and planking used in today's bridges.

Occasionally, the Stedman family would host a dance on a large redwood stump. These stumps were often up to ten feet in diameter. One stump near their home was eight feet above the ground. In order to participate in the Stedman dance, couples had to climb up a ladder to reach the flat stump surface. Fortunately, no one fell off the dance floor in the dances, which were often like square dances. In 1874 the North Pacific Railroad was being built from Sausalito to Tomales.

Late in the afternoon of April 19, 1875, on their way home from San Rafael, the father and son were thrown out of their buggy. The high-spirited young mare was spooked by an empty rice sack that a gust of wind blew upward from the road. Stephen was unhurt. Robert Stedman went down a thirty-foot embankment and across the entrance to the White's Hill Tunnel. His spine was severed as he fell on one the rails laid upon ties his company had provided the North Pacific Railroad. Declining being moved to a nearby neighbor's house, he died in the arms of the son he was closest to; the pair had worked together since 1854. It was a tragic end to the life of one of northern California's true pioneers.

---

[389] *Ibid.*, p. 14.

[390] *Ibid.*, p. 15.

CHAPTER 11

Edward Chever, Yuba
City Pioneer Settler

A young and rather pretty squaw came and talked to me with greatest animation. She put her hand next to mine as if fascinated by the contrast in color. Then she held up her baby for inspection and admiration, and at last, using signs, asked me for the oilcloth coat I was wearing. As it had a long rent in the back it seemed a small gift to bestow, but its possession made her happy.

—March 30, 1850, at an Indian encampment on land in the
Straits of Magellan

As it did in Chile, throughout Central and South America, and even across the planet from Western Europe to Australia and China, gold fever spread like an epidemic of the heart, mind, and soul. Wherever newspapers existed with a reading public, the idea of getting rich found a ready audience. During the spring and through the remainder of 1848, the itch for riches spread like a plague from Sutter's little lumber sawmill on the American River in the hills northeast of Sutter's Mill to the far corners of an entire planet. This was a phenomenon without precedent in the world.

One of the hundreds of thousands swept up by this pandemic was a young adventurous Illinois farmer named Edward G. Chever. The sodbuster held one slight, but nonetheless real, advantage over many other forty-niners: he had two brothers already in California—although until he arrived in San Francisco, Chever had no idea where they were. Chever made almost daily entries in his diary. Born and raised with his brothers in Salem, Massachusetts, Chever had emigrated to Illinois before traveling east again to Boston to embark for San

Francisco on an ocean voyage to California—probably the safest route, yet one of the longest and slowest.

Chever's ship was the *Saltillo,* which was a midsized vessel that he described as "less than three-hundred ton, brig."[391] The *Saltillo* was the first passenger ship to sail from Boston to California. Edward was one of only twelve passengers. Unfortunately for all on board, the captain had a drinking problem. It wasn't long before a struggle to control the ship broke out between the first mate and the captain. This conflict soon brought on a high level of tension in which passengers (including Chever) and all the crewmen shared. One of their diversions was to view numerous sea lions, flocks of sea birds, penguins, and whales, which made life on board barely tolerable.

"Land ho!" rang out from the lookout atop the main mast soon after dinner was served on March 15, 1849. All twelve passengers clambered over one another to be the first on deck in spite of the strong wind that was blowing. Chever wrote, "In my eagerness I climbed to the main top."[392]

The captain had to approach the straits cautiously because the winds were at gale force. "Cape Virgins it is, a tall mountain with precipitous sides three hundred feet high."[393] Just after the ship was safely anchored, a squall blew up, and the crew suffered from being on duty for forty-eight hours straight.

Due to the constant stress of the long hours, tempers reached the boiling point when a sailor misunderstood a captain's order. The ship almost hit a shoal. Infuriated by what he'd misinterpreted as disobedience, the captain took out two pistols to threaten three of the crew, who by now had decided to openly defy his orders. Fortunately, high winds ended the dispute by blowing the ship to safety offshore. At last the ship anchored again, this time safely. Chever recalled what happened next.

---

[391] Edward E. Chever, "Through the Straits of Magellan in 1849," *Quarterly of the Society of California Pioneers* 4 (September 30, 1927), 127. The brig reached Sacramento by way of San Francisco. See Sacramento's *Placer Times,* August 11, 1849, which reported, "Just arrived ... brig *Saltillo* from Boston. And now landing opposite Hansley, Reading."

[392] *Ibid.,* p. 137.

[393] *Ibid.,* p. 138.

Mason, son of one of the owners of the brig, and I talked over the trouble and its cause in the morning. On deck was a cask of sherry which we had found floating at sea, also a demijohn of brandy. We emptied both, and as the weather continued stormy, remained at anchor all day. The sailors were returned to duty. That day a vessel flying the French flag came out from the Second Narrows and sailed on toward the Atlantic.[394]

To the mostly American passengers, the southeastern coast of South America appeared barren and almost uninhabited. As the weather cleared a bit, the crew began raising its anchors, but their lines had fouled. New anchors were lowered and set in place to securely hold the ship. A boat was lowered so that six passengers could do a bit of exploring. In the meantime, those already ashore gathered berries and shot a number of ducks and geese, which added much to their menu. The next day, the *Anthem,* a schooner out of New York that had sailed twenty days after the *Saltillo* had departed from Boston, approached the *Saltillo* so it could anchor nearby.

Talking to the *Anthem*'s passengers helped Chever identify a second schooner that they had also spotted, the *Iowa.* This third American ship originated in Sag Harbor, New York, the easternmost village on the end of Long Island.

Chever was impressed by the variety of gold seekers on the *Iowa,* despite a sore tooth that had begun troubling him.

Nothing but an El Dorado could have drawn such a curious crowd so far away from home. One man wearing a long drab coat and slouch hat with an indescribable comic air had been the skipper of a down east sloop. There were several professional looking gentlemen who wore glasses, some who shaved clean, and more who had full beards, and one boy with bright blue eyes and light hair seemed to be there by accident. Best of all we saw newspapers published since we had left home that confirmed the stories of the gold discoveries.[395]

---

[394] *Ibid.,* o. 141.
[395] Ibid., p. 143.

In sight of each other, the three American ships began passing through the straits. First they went into Saint Nicholas Bay and Fortesque Bay. There, they observed a mountain that was almost completely bare of vegetation and "a fringe of trees tangled with vines and sheltering many varieties of beautiful and delicate flowers."[396]

On March 30, Chever went ashore and wrote,

> We came upon an Indian camp infested with numerous snapping dogs. The huts were constructed of a framework of saplings, the heavy ends of which were secured in the ground, while the pliant tops were bent in and bound together and the whole covered with seal skins.
>
> Their smoking ceremony, for ceremony it was, was curious. When the pipe had been filled all the bucks formed a circle, sitting on the ground. The first one to smoke placed a live coal on the pipe, then drew the smoke into his mouth and swallowed it. Closing his eyes and bending his head forward he passed the lighted pipe to the buck next to him. Thus the pipe went to all in turn. It was not offered to me, however. A young and rather pretty squaw came and talked to me with greatest animation. She put her hand next to mine as if fascinated by the contrast in color. Then she held up her baby for inspection and admiration, and at last, using signs, asked me for the oilcloth coat I was wearing. As it had a long rent in the back it seemed a small gift to bestow, but its possession made her happy.[397]

This is only one of several recorded incidences where there was a friendly contact and interchange between Indians and forty-niners. Chever's oilcloth coat was worth more to the Indian woman than it was to him. They had been making some progress through the straits, but Chever was anxious to go faster.

On Sunday, April 9, the crew sighted the steamer *Panama*. It too was headed

---

[396] Ibid., p.144.
[397] Ibid., pp. 145–146.

to San Francisco. Sensing the chance to speed up the slow-moving *Saltillo,* the captain offered to pay five hundred dollars to the *Panama's* captain to tow the *Saltillo* out to the Pacific. The *Panama's* captain said he lacked the authority to comply with the request and turned down the offer. However, the passengers obtained newspapers dated February 17, 1849, from passengers on the *Panama.*

The next day was particularly important for Chever. The wind changed suddenly, which caused the captain to double back on their course for safety. They anchored in Borja Bay and were joined there by three other American ships: two schooners, the *Empire* and the *Sea Witch* from New York, and the pilot boat *Anonyma* from Boston. Chever and a few other passengers visited both of the other vessels when they anchored nearby. Originally, the *Sea Witch* had been built to be a fishing smack, yet its well was closed off and its hold caulked, which later served as its kitchen and dining area.

Immediately, Chever made an offer to the skipper of the *Sea Witch,* Captain Lewis, to become the ship's second passenger. Chever had become increasingly impatient at being stuck on board the slow-moving *Saltilla.* He and Captain Lewis came to an agreement on a fair passage price to San Francisco. The *Sea Witch* could sail faster because she weighed just one hundred tons. On April 11 a third schooner, the *Velasco,* appeared.[398] Not long after this, the vessels all sailed into Tamar Harbor. They were only about thirty miles east of the Pacific Ocean. Chever's diary described a dramatic series of events. Other ships had near fatal accidents, and Chever was amazed by the terrible roughness of the seas.

> Sunday, April 15, all the vessels sailed further into the Harbor to secure safer anchorage. On Monday we got underway at noon. The *Velasco* and the *Iowa* overtook us, the former had struck the rocks and lost part of her keel and one man on the *Iowa* had his leg broken ... We were all compelled to keep under sail until morning when we were off Cape Pillar, the western extremity of the Straits. The sea was terribly rough. When we were in the hollow of the waves we could hardly see the tops of the mountains above the water.[399]

---

[398] Ibid., p. 149.
[399] Ibid., p. 150.

At last away from the Straits of Magellan and in open ocean again, the little *Sea Witch* was ahead of the other ships.

> As the breeze freshened, the *Sea Witch* seemed to leap from wave to wave. The next morning we were alone on the blue ocean, neither land nor sails to be seen, and our craft skimming over its surface like a sea-bird. We were accompanied by numbers of Cape Pigeons (Stormy Petrols), and occasionally an Albatross circled and wheeled in easy flight, borne lightly on wide extended wings.[400]

This had to have been one of those moments at sea when all on board felt at least some relief. For more than a month, they had felt trapped by high winds and dangerous shoals within the straits. They were free again.

Chever described taking his meals inside of the boat's tiny hold on a semicircular board with cleats to help hold dishes in place as the ship veered sharply from side to side and up and down. His trunk served as the base for the table after it was swung down from the ceiling at mealtimes. Between meals, the table or board was held up by a hook. The crackers were old, and weevils had taken possession of and woven webs in them.

For Chever and his fellow passenger, it was a blessing that Captain Lewis was an experienced captain. On June 15, after just fifty-four days at sea from the straits, they passed through the Golden Gate. Chever was relieved to see a harbor pilot come on board. He told him one of his brothers, David (who went by the name of Gus), was awaiting him in San Francisco.

Chever's description of early San Francisco is a straightforward snapshot of California's only real port, which was rapidly building.

> It was a strange place to a newcomer at that time. Passengers were rowed ashore in a boat, and jumped from the bow to a sand beach where Montgomery Street is now [in January 1891]. Brush covered the land, or rather sand hills, between Kearny and Dupont Streets near Sacramento [Street].[401]

---

[400] Ibid.,p. 150.
[401] Ibid., p. 151.

This simple description might well strike someone today as odd and archaic if one stood about where Chever once was on Montgomery Street, because one would be dwarfed by giant concrete, steel, and plate glass windows. Let's return to Edward Chever's first impression of San Francisco.

> In fact, the winds swept across a series of sand hills with such force that at times the sand was driven in clouds along the main traveled roads. I noticed that horse shoes and pieces of metal lying on the surface were smooth and brightly burnished by the attrition of the sand.[402]

Despite the ill effects of sand blasts, due to its excellent natural harbor, San Francisco held its position as California's primary seaport throughout the nineteenth and early twentieth centuries. The change of its foremost city thoroughfare from Montgomery Street to Market Street by its city planner and surveyor, Jasper O'Farrell, was barely two years old.[403]

In part because time was money, Chever, like almost all of his fellow forty-niners, only stayed only a few days in San Francisco.

> There were a considerable number of adobe houses, many built of wood, but more numerous were cloth structures and tents. None of the houses had the appearance of homes. Stores and saloons were everywhere.[404]

He went on to note something that remains as relevant about today's city as it was in 1849.

> And such a mixture of races! There were no mosquitoes in the more settled portion of the town, but fleas abounded, savage,

---

[402] *Ibid.*, p. 151.

[403] See Frank Baumgardner, *Blood Will Tell: Divvying up Early California from Colonel Juan Bautista De Anza to Jasper O'Farrell* (North Charleston, SC: CreateSpace Independent Publishing Platform, 2014), pp. 84ff.

[404] *Ibid.*, p. 151.

bloodthirsty, seemingly insatiate. There was no escape from them and their elusiveness, when hunted, was exasperating.[405]

He continued to note,

> The harbor at that time was a forest of masts. Not only had vessels arrived from Atlantic ports, but from South America, Mexico and the islands of the Pacific Ocean every available craft had sailed to California, and as each anchored in the Bay, all her sailors started for the gold diggings.[406]

The lack of crewmen became so critical that at one point, one captain put his crew in irons when the ship anchored in San Francisco Harbor. Chever saw people dressed differently than anything he'd seen on the East Coast. Someone dressed very shabbily did not mean what it might mean there.

> The people you met could not be classified by difference of dress. Everyone depended on himself for the carrying of his trunk or the protection of his person. A request made to a stranger to perform some menial service might lead to a fight. A roughly dressed man might consider himself a millionaire.[407]

Almost everyone Chever saw in San Francisco seemed to be in a rush to get to the mines. The former fishing boat, the *Sea Witch*, made another transformation from a seagoing vessel to river packet, departing on June 20, 1849, and sailing east across the bay. In its initial trip from San Francisco to Sacramento Captain Lewis crammed 147 passengers, baggage, mining equipment, and crew on board. Most of the passengers slept out on deck, which mightily upset Watch, the ship's dog, a Newfoundland, who had to stumble over snoring bodies as well as much baggage.

---

[405] *Ibid.,* p. 152.
[406] *Ibid.,* pp. 152–153.
[407] *Ibid.,* p. 153.

When the *Sea Witch* ran aground for the second time, still a good distance from Sacramento, Gus and his brother launched their own whale boat. A few others left with them. If there had been no mosquitoes in San Francisco, the Sacramento River Delta more than made up for it by making their hard work of rowing even harder. As they heaved away at their oars, they noted many fish, a mountain lion, and many glass bottles. Chever was amazed at how much broken glass was crushed into macadam by settlers' wagons and carts in the towns, including the small town of Sacramento. Using their sail, they passed Sutterville, a town which has since disappeared. Chever also spotted many eagles, other vessels headed upstream, several large ships tied up near the shore, and a garrison of army troopers.

As they entered Sacramento City, they saw a group of Californios struggling to drive a herd of cattle across the river.

> A funny sight greeted us. Some Californians were ferrying wild cattle across the river, and were dashing through the brush trying to escape them, caught sight of a red-shirted American (all the Americans wore red shirts) and there were some fast running for the nearest tree. The Californians were magnificent horsemen, their motion of throwing the lasso was exceedingly graceful. The Californians would manage the steer like a plaything, seemingly running away from him, with one motion of his hand throwing him heavily to the ground.[408]

Now in Sacramento for the first time, Chever noted that the first store there had been founded by King James of William. The brothers visited it, which was not far from the Embarcadero or wharf. They discovered that their other brother, Henry, had a room at Sutter's Fort. As soon as they could, they found the room and got their first good night of sleep they'd had since leaving San Francisco. As they bedded down for the night, they learned from an old Californio that Sacramento's (or "Sacramento City's"[409]) original name was

---

[408] *Ibid.,* p. 156.

[409] Other forty-niners, including Israel Hale, usually referred to the eventual state capital as Sacramento City.

Sutter's Embarcadero. It was late June, and the temperature there read 103 degrees in the shade, a typical heat wave in the San Joaquin Valley. Cool nights soon revived them. One of the Donners ran a restaurant. Andres Pico, brother of the last Mexican governor, Pio Pico, took them to lunch there. He proudly displayed a silver relic, a gun that the Prince of Wales had bestowed to the native Hawaiian king. Californios like Pico were generous to newcomers.

They planned to hire Indians to row them to Hock Farm. When none of the Indians showed up, their visit was delayed. Chever described the Fourth of July celebration. He saluted the "ladies" of 1849 California in this way.

> The evening of the 3rd of July was celebrated by setting off such fireworks as we could buy or manufacture for the occasion. A keg of gunpowder was fired by means of a fuse, but the report was less than we expected. The Fourth was devoted to drinking. Sober men were scarce before noon. The great event of the season was the grand ball that night in the house near the center of the fort. Henry A. Schoolcraft acted as the Master of Ceremonies. Some of the ladies came nearly a hundred miles to participate.[410]

The next day, they finally got underway, sometimes using the whale boat's sail and at other times having to depend on hired Indians to row. Chever remarked about again being bothered by mosquitoes and how clear the water was, first in the Sacramento and later in the Feather River. They passed town sites that had been set up for Vernon and Fremont before reaching the mouth of the Feather River. It was hard work rowing against the swifter moving current of the Feather. First they reached the settler, Nicolaus Alger, and then Hock Farm as darkness began to fall at five o'clock.

Chever took the time to pay homage to John Sutter,

> Captain Sutter and his son came out to meet us, the Captain apologizing for the roughness of his accommodations. He invited us to occupy rooms in his house, but we assured him

---

[410] *Ibid.*, p. 157.

that we had every convenience for camping. Captain Sutter told us that since the discovery of gold in California he had received letters of inquiry from all parts of Europe and America, and that hundreds of letters of introduction were constantly being handed to him. He said that this visit from old friends [Chever's party included James King of William, Henry A. Schoolcraft, Major Jacob R. Snyder, as well as the three Chever brothers.] was very pleasing, and he was pleased to call us old friends. We were invited to take supper with him in the house and accepted his invitation ... After supper we went in the Captain's room to pass the evening in describing Captain Sutter I should say that he was about five feet seven inches tall, rather stout and somewhat bald. He had a high forehead, blue eyes and wore a moustache and imperial. [411] He was very hospitable. We enjoyed his description of early days in Missouri and California and his reminiscences of noted men who had been his guests at the fort. It was late when we retired and we slept comfortably in the dooryard. After breakfast the whole party except myself started for Sacramento. Captain Sutter had been expecting to go there before we came.[412]

Because Edward Chever wasn't well-known to Sutter, he had to accept what the captain and his staff at Hock Farm assigned him. For the next few days, Chever had been assigned to ride a fractious horse that continually tried to buck him and that anyone would have had trouble controlling. Chever somehow pushed the nag along the trail that led to the future site of Yuba City. Already he was turning over employment options in his mind as he made his way back down the Feather River to Sacramento. A number of Chileans shared the boat with him.

After his return to Sacramento, his toothache returned with a vengeance.

---

[411] An imperial is defined as "a small pointed beard growing below the lower lip (associated with Napoleon III of France."*Concise Oxford English Dictionary*, 11th edition, eds. Catherine Soanes and Angus Stevenson.

[412] Ibid., p. 159.

I called on Dr. Cragan in Sacramento and survived the torment
of having a tooth twisted from its socket by one who never could
become a dentist. His fee, however, was equal to the rest of the
suffering—one half an ounce, eight dollars![413]

Whether or not "Dr. Cragan" had ever had any real dental training is
unknown; there were many quacks who tormented the forty-niners. We can
only imagine how much pain Edward went through during the "good old days"
before anesthetics. As he recovered the best he could, he heard that the *Saltillo*,
like the *Sea Witch*, had just arrived from San Francisco. It brought the latest
news that only the steamer from Panama could bring regarding the rest of the
United States,

> Cholera is raging in the States, and there were several cases on
> board the steamer. Great fire in St. Louis, New Orleans under
> water. The partisans of Forrest and Macready [MacReedy or
> McReady?] have organized a Vigilance Committee to protect
> the community from the depredations of the Hounds who have
> been a scourge [to San Francisco] since last winter.[414]

The national news update came like a gift from the heavens to Crever
and his lonely brothers, who were so far from the existing states. This news
update was among his final diary entries. It was written in July 1849, before
some others of the newcomers in this book had arrived in the diggings. From
Sacramento, Chever visited Coloma, Greenwood Valley, and Grass Valley. At
this point, he joined a group of Oregon miners to do some surface mining. His
journal noted that he was joined by two sons of Judge Blackburn from Santa
Cruz. "Our party averaged two ounces of gold to each man during the time we
worked on our claim."[415] He stopped mining to travel up to Yuba City, where
white settlement had begun.

---

[413] Ibid., p. 159.
[414] *Ibid.*, p. 162.
[415] *Ibid.*, p. 162.

I rode to Yuba City, where Tolman H. Rolfe and my brother, Gus, had started a store, and I became the third white settler in Yuba City in September, 1849. The name Yuba on the original was spelled Yubu. It was intended to preserve the Indian name. The Indians pronounced it "Yubum" and called Sutter's place [Hock Farm] Hockem, but the Americans shortened those names to Yuba and Hock.[416]

During the winter of 1849–1850, setting up and operating their store and even keeping it standing was a struggle that very nearly ended their enterprise and any hope of their remaining in California. The following description was duplicated many times by other newcomers during these first two years of the gold rush.

The store was made of posts set close together in the ground. There were covered with canvas, which passing over a ridge pole, formed the roof. The rain moistened the earth that supported the posts forming the sides of the structure. It also loosened the pins which secured my tent, so I was awakened in the night by the falling of my tent and it was some time before I could get out from under the wet canvas. On entering the store I found that the side was being pushed over by the wind. This structure was our last chance for shelter, and our total population of three stood an animated braces with our shoulders against the house and toward the storm. Several times we were crowded backward by severe gusts of wind, but we managed to hold the house up until daylight when we made it safe by use of guy-ropes.[417]

During the winter, a great many more Americans who were greenhorn miners arrived from across the plains. Many who were in Yuba City during the winter of 1849–1850 didn't remain long. There were a sufficient number of them that three small steamers, the *Lawrence,* the *Linda,* and later the *El Dorado,*

---

[416] *Ibid.,* p. 162.
[417] *Ibid.,* p. 163.

made regular runs from San Francisco to Yuba City. Many structures went up: hotels, saloons, gambling halls, and houses.

Looking back on his sea voyage and his first year in California, Edward Chever addressed early members of the Society of California Pioneers at the Palace Hotel on January 13, 1891. "It was my fortune to be one of the passengers on board the *Saltillo,* a medium sized, less than 300 tons brig."[418] There were others present who could remember what the gold rush was like because they too were participants. Many who were forty-niners did not remain in California. As Chever summarized his experience in putting Yuba City on California's map, he stated with justifiable pride, "For a time the 'city' [Yuba City] bade fair to become the third largest city in the state."[419]

---

[418] Ibid., p. 1.
[419] Ibid., p. 163.

CHAPTER 12

Alonzo Delano Humorist, Pioneer, Grass Valley Treasurer

I inquired by signs if he was sick. He put his hand just back of his ear, and signified that he had been in such pain that he had not slept for two nights. Feeling the spot indicated, I found a tumor gathering, when returning to my house, I got some strong volatile liniment, with which I rubbed the affected part well, and giving him a pretty good pill of opium, I directed him to get to bed, assuring him that then he would sleep. When morning came, the swelling had nearly subsided, and he felt much better.[420]

—Delano's description of his administration of a salve to a California Indian chief's head, 1849

The Empire State sent many adventurous gold seekers to California during the gold rush. Alonzo Delano hailed from upstate New York. He was born on July 2, 1806, in Aurora, Erie County, New York. Alonzo's father, Dr. Frederick Delano, was what today is called a general practitioner or family practice physician. Dr. Delano also was among the first settlers of the town; his family was descended from French Huguenots. Phillipe de la Noye was Alonzo's great-great-grandfather and also was the great-great-great-great-grandfather of the thirty-second US president, Franklin Delano Roosevelt.

As a child, Alonzo observed his father's medical practice, and he carried on his father's compassionate caring for his fellow man in California, although he wasn't a physician with a MD degree. Soon after his arrival in northern

---

[420] *Ibid.*, p. 129.

California, Delano made use of his medical knowledge to aid a suffering Indian chief.

Alonzo grew up among nine siblings. He struck out on his own by leaving school when he was fifteen. He moved west, at first to Indiana and then Ohio and Illinois. He succeeded in business as a merchant, selling whiskey, silk goods, lard, and bank stocks. Although his work took him west, he maintained contact with his family and friends in New York. There, he fell in love and married Mary Burt in New York State in 1830. The couple moved first to Indiana and later to Ottawa, in northcentral Illinois, where they had two children, Fred (1833–1857) and Harriet (b. 1843). Alonzo and his wife were separated when he went to California. She would return to New York to be with their son, Fred, who became an invalid. After Fred's death in 1857, Mary moved to Grass Valley, where she lived with Alonzo until her death in 1871.

By 1848, following the westward march of the pioneers, he relocated to the town of Ottawa, Illinois. He nearly died from consumption during the same year. His doctor advised him to go to California for his health and to get more exercise. As he started planning his cross-country trek, Delano made deals to send dispatches from the trail to the *Ottawa Free Trader* and to the *True Delta* in New Orleans.

It was no easy task making the overland journey to the northern California gold region. Numerous travelers succumbed, and their bodies were left beside the trail in shallow graves. After arriving in the High Sierra, Delano became a humorist and sketch writer, portraying gold rush mining camps. Going by the pen name "Old Block," from 1853 to 1857, Delano created a series of short, witty stories that rivaled those of Mark Twain and Bret Harte in popularity. Some of his colorful characters are presented in this chapter, along with excerpts from Delano's eyewitness account of his steps and missteps along the Oregon and California Trails.[421]

In his lengthy, accurate book, *Across the Plains and among the Diggings*, published in 1853, Delano began with a description of his feelings when gold fever first struck. On April 5, 1849, he wrote, "On that day I became a nomad

---

[421] Wikipedia, accessed December 19–20, 2915.

denizen of the world, a new and important era in my life."[422] While preparing to leave Ottawa, Illinois, his most recent home, he bought what others thought were the essentials to make the tough journey across the continent: supplies, a wagon, and cattle. The Dayton Company's plan was to meet in St. Joseph, Missouri. They elected a leader, "Captain" Jesse Greene. Traveling first by the steamer *Revolution* down the Mississippi to St. Louis, Delano transferred his goods to the riverboat *Embassy,* filled to overflowing and bound for St. Joseph, Missouri. When he arrived there, Delano took some time to repair his wagon. Other members of his Ottawa Company left without him. While falling asleep one night, he began feeling "cold." His clear description of how a cholera victim feels followed.

As Delano started suffering, a friend he had met earlier, Harris, died of cholera. Fortunately, Delano was taken in and cared for by a caring individual named Mr. Van Leuvin, and he quickly recovered. By May 2, he was strong enough to ride his pony, Old Shabanay, to the ferry twelve miles from St. Joseph, where he learned his party had just left earlier that day. Although he was slowed by his cattle that needed green grass, at least Delano's health had returned. He returned to the saddle again.

What makes Alonzo Delano's memoir especially memorable is the fact that he included many small details omitted by other forty-niners who kept diaries. They had to write abbreviated accounts because they didn't have time to write complete accounts of all their trials and tribulations. In addition, unlike most forty-niners, Delano had decided (possibly even before he'd left Illinois) that if he survived the perilous cross-country journey to the California mines, he wasn't about to return to the Midwest or New York.

Mishaps and mistakes almost doomed him several times. On September 3, 1848, his party was on a ridge overlooking the Humboldt River. As he descended to the valley and climbed over some rocks, he lost his "revolver, which probably dropped from my pocket."[423] He was lucky the gun didn't go off because it might have killed or injured him or someone else. By the time he realized it was

---

[422] See Alonzo Delano, *Across the Plains and among the Diggings: A Reprint of the Original Edition with Numerous Reproductions Taken by Louis Palenske, and Foreword and Epilogue by Rufus Rockwell Wilson* (New York: Wilson-Erickson, Inc., 1936), 1.

[423] *Ibid.,* p. 94.

missing, it was too late to go back to look for it. At the same time, their party learned from members of a mule train on its way east that they were still 250 miles away from the California mines. The following day, they heard about a battle that had occurred between Indians and whites "a few days before," when the Indians "had driven off all the cattle belonging to a man who had a family with him." According to Captain King, the leader of the posse formed to pursue the Indians, who reported what happened next.

> His party had not gone far, when, on turning around a rock, they came in contact with four Indians, who at once drew their bows. Each man selected his antagonist, and a desperate fight for life commenced. Elliott wounded his man mortally, though he commenced a flight. Moore had also wounded his, but he still continued to discharge his arrows before Moore could reload, who, to avoid the arrows, beat his head, but was severely wounded while King, after wounding his, advanced, and after a desperate conflict dispatched him with his knife, after firing his pistol.[424]

Before the Indian was killed. he still managed to shoot many arrows at Captain King. One grazed King's head, but he survived.

Others who were part of Delano's party, according to Delano's entry of September 14, 1849, were "Hittle, Tuttle, and Jackson."[425] On the same day, Delano wrote about a "poor fellow who got lost while hunting and was out six days without eating."[426] He became so dazed and disoriented that at first, when members of Delano's party approached him, he began to try to "fly." Eventually he calmed down. They took him back to their wagons and fed him. That same night, he "became perfectly composed." Shortly thereafter, the "poor fellow" safely departed from Delano's party. He caught up with his own party, which was some "thirty miles" ahead on the trail.[427]

---

[424] *Ibid.,* p. 94.

[425] *Ibid.,* p. 99.

[426] *Ibid.,* p. 99.

[427] *Ibid.,* pp. 99–100.

As the summer of 1849 waned, Delano and his party were near California territory. Before reaching the outskirts of Sacramento, the emigrant had another near death experience. He nearly died in a brush with two bears. On September 16, he noted, "Spent much of the day striding fast to catch up with *Colonel Watkins*."[428] They were still walking through rough desert. Two of Watkins' men walked over some hills with a pail to get the party some water. Meanwhile, Delano marched twenty-five miles in one day. He was moving along as fast as he could. The forty-two-year-old was anxious to reach the California mines.

Although he omitted the exact date, Delano arrived in Sacramento, seeing it for the first time. He had only four dollars to his name. He was well aware that it would take at least two hundred dollars to buy the required mining tools. Fortunately for him, he met a group of friends, including his original leader, Captain Jesse Greene, as well as three others, "Dr. Hall," "Mr. Rood," and "Dr. M. B. Angel." These men staked him the funds to start his mining career. Delano's comment was, "I was more rejoiced to see them than they possibly could have been to see me."[429]

As only a newcomer could do, Delano clearly described the town of Sacramento. No one then had a clue, much less knew for sure, that about thirty years later, this "forest of tents" would become the eventual capital city of the state.

The almost penniless greenhorn noted Sacramento had what he called "a floating population of about five thousand."[430] Surveyors had plotted out the town "in the spring of 1849, on the east bank of the Sacramento River, less than one eighth of a mile wide."[431] Looking back when he published his memoir in 1853, Delano saw that some Sacramento lots that had originally sold for two hundred dollars were selling for thirty thousand dollars. If one had the money to buy a lot and hold onto it for even a few years, the investment paid off handsomely.

Pushing onward generally toward the northwest from Sacramento, Delano passed Bidwell's Bar, a part of which was called "Dawlytown, named after a

---

[428] *Ibid.,* p. 101.

[429] *Ibid.,* p. 101.

[430] *Ibid.,* p. 104.

[431] *Ibid.,* pp. 109–110.

young merchant who first opened a store on this point, about two months before."[432] By November, Delano found himself on the Yuba River, the place to be if one was a forty-niner. Along the way, he was aided by an elderly California gentleman who lit a fire as a beacon, which Delano followed. The two paused to share a dinner alongside the trail. As they shared breakfast the next day, Delano discovered the man had once been "a student of my father—Dr. Frederick Delano of Aurora, New York."[433] Coming across this man who hailed from Delano's home town was unusual but not unheard of in the early gold country.

On November 3, as he was within four miles of the Yuba River, it began to rain heavily. It was the first rain of the rainy season, which was actually a bit late in the year for northern California. He almost lost his life as well as his wagon while getting across the Yuba.

At the same time, he had another near death experience. "I was taken with the cholera, and came within an ace of slipping my wind."[434] He began vomiting and couldn't find anyone who knew as much as he did himself, having grown up in a doctor's family. He knew the treatment he needed was calomel, camphor, and opium to ease the severe pain he had in his stomach and intestinal tract. The poorly trained "doctor" forced him to take "Number Six," some concoction that, if anything, made him sicker. He felt like his insides were burning. He called out so loudly that others in the camp became alarmed. Finally, after the patient called for "brandy, fire, turpentine, live coals," the "doctor" finally poured out half a glass of brandy, which in fact, was only more concentrated "Number Six."

Finally, just as Delano thought that he was surely done for, somehow the latest dose of frontier medicine stuck. The man then gave him the calomel, camphor, and opium, which also stayed down. The forty-two-year-old storekeeper began improving at last.

When there was a break in the rains in February or March 1850, Delano moved back from the mountains into Dawlytown.

Soon after that, a fight broke out between some Indians and the miners, which did not end well for the Indians. Delano related what happened. One of

---

[432] *Ibid.*, p. 112.

[433] *Ibid.*, p. 114.

[434] *Ibid.*, p. 115.

the Indians stole an ax from the tent of a miner. The Indian village was only a mile or two away. When the miner went to the village and used coarse language demanding the return of the ax, another Indian went into a wigwam, retrieved the ax, and gave it back to the miner. Instead of simply taking it and leaving, the miner began to beat the Indian. When he finally turned to go, the Indian retaliated by grabbing his bow and shooting the miner in the back. Soon after this, another miner was killed with an Indian arrow when the miner and a friend were hunting for lost mules. A third problem, related to the first two, was that the Indians had run off with some horses and cattle. As a result of these incidents, which the miners often called "outrages," the miners organized a posse that went back to the village, shooting and killing five or six Indians.

Such terrifying incidents struck fear into the hearts of Indians and miners alike. As an educated American from pioneer roots, Delano's early education and upbringing as the son of an upstate New York doctor came into play. He finished making plans to receive merchandise for sale to the miners in the area around Grass Valley, and he reached out in a unique way to the nearest tribe of California Indians, whose chief was suffering from a serious skin "tumor."

> Soon after I got my house, erected, mercantile and housekeeping arrangements completed, I strolled one evening into the village, and saw the chief sitting by the fire in front of his house, apparently suffering from pain. I inquired by signs if he was sick. He put his hand just back of his ear, and signified that he had been in such pain that he had not slept for two nights. Feeling the spot indicated, I found a tumor gathering, when returning to my house, I got some strong volatile liniment, with which I rubbed the affected part well, and giving him a pretty good pill of opium, I directed him to get to bed, assuring him that then he would sleep. When morning came, the swelling had nearly subsided, and he felt much better.[435]

Certainly Delano was not the only forty-niner who had difficulties communicating with the Indians. As the preceding incident from Delano's

---

[435] *Ibid.*, p. 129.

life indicates, he was a perceptive, caring American whose actions made him a favored resident and friend of the Indians. He noted that at any time, they could have stolen goods from his supply, yet they never did. Occasionally when Delano had to be absent for a day or so, Indians from this tribe watched over merchandise in his store. Other Indians stole items when they saw an opportunity from other forty-niners who, unlike Delano, were aliens or acted in a hostile manner to them.

On March 29, 1850, Delano returned to Dawlyville. When the Feather River water at his claim continued to be too high for anyone to work, Delano went to Marysville, where he hoped he could get into some kind of work that might help him get by. At this point, he had just thirty-two dollars to his name, enough for about a week of board there. Because he knew he could draw, he took along "some crayons and drawing paper."[436] Putting his talents to work, he made four hundred dollars in three weeks drawing portraits of miners and selling them.

During the same spring, some miners discovered that a few head of their oxen were missing. About fifteen men set out on a mission of revenge. As soon as they arrived at the Indian village, they surrounded it. Many of the Indians tried to escape, but fifteen were shot dead.

While they were still celebrating the success of their revenge on their way back to their camp, their sense of justice was a little shaken, by seeing every ox which they had supposed stolen quietly feeding in a somewhat isolated gorge. The oxen had strayed in search of grass. [437]

This wasn't the first or only time a mistake by either the miners or the Indians led to unnecessary shootings, injuries, and deaths of innocent victims. In the following instance, it was a case of "an eye for eye" gone wrong.

Nevertheless, it was a tragic incident that easily could have led to far more than fifteen innocent dead. When Grass Valley, in Nevada County, was during its earliest settlement phase, two brothers named Holt established a sawmill outside the little town. The pair gave small presents to the Indians. Soon they acquired a good reputation among both miners and local Indians. However,

---

[436] *Ibid.,* p. 127.
[437] *Ibid.,* p. 137.

another white man living nearby, whose name Delano did not know or simply omitted, held an Indian woman against her will in his cabin. He repeatedly forced her to have sex with him for two days and nights. When at last she escaped, she fled to her tribe. The angry Indians went out but couldn't find the guilty white man; he had left the area. Intent on vengeance, some of the Indians surrounded the kindly sawmill owner one morning. They murdered him. Before dying, he called out to warn his brother, who fled the scene. The other brother escaped but was wounded by two arrows.[438]

The surviving brother escaped the Indians and took refuge at the cabin of Judge Walsh. Word went out about the attack, and three other miners and the judge armed themselves in preparation for an imminent Indian attack. Fortunately, it never came. As he concluded his description, Delano couldn't resist commenting, "The crime of one man caused another white man to be killed and the injury of his brother. Also it had nearly caused the deaths of many." Reversing the picture, in Delano's words, "Had the outrage been perpetrated by an Indian on a white woman, her kindred would quite as likely have taken a revenge on the whole tribe, by killing or driving them off."[439]

Before turning to other matters, Delano related another anecdote from his own life in early northern California that illustrated how much the settlers depended on each other. It was a relationship that could involve risks and even personal danger. After Delano obtained a plot of land for a store, another white man named Gray moved in next to him. Gray sometimes joked with some of the Indians, but other Indians disliked him because of his volatile temper. Delano had to make a trip to Marysville and left his store to Gray to run. Gray foolishly gave some of the Indians liquor. When they returned wanting more, Gray drove them away and then left. On the second day, in the evening, Delano returned at about nine o'clock.

Indians who had befriended Delano held his bridle, gave him some water, unsaddled his horse, and led the horse off to where there was grass. After going into the store and striking a light, Delano caught sight of an Indian sliding out the back door. Delano heard the sound of liquid running, discovered the plug

---

438 *Ibid.*, p. 137.
439 *Ibid.*, p. 137.

was pulled out of the brandy cask, and saw brandy draining into a bucket. He plugged the cask and poured the bandy back into it. Delano immediately informed the chief "that he had a bad Indian"[440] and turned in for the night. Gray was surprised that Delano could fall asleep under the circumstances.

Delano got caught up in a new wave of gold excitement that broke out in May 1850. The myth reached Grass Valley that there was a gold lake some one hundred miles up into the Sierra Nevada Mountains, where gold pebbles lay for the taking on the shores of the lake. Delano followed the miners and set up another branch of his store. "Some dug down forty or fifty feet and they explored till the highest ridge of the Sierra was passed."[441] As was the case for the entire gold rush, a few prospered, but most failed and went home with nothing. By the fall of 1850, Delano gave up any further land speculation to concentrate on building a new store up at Gold Lake. He and his associate, Brinkerhoff, organized a mule pack train carrying their goods. By the end of 1850, he had to give it up, losing about one thousand dollars in the process.[442]

Jumping back for a moment, in June 1850, Independence Bar, in the High Sierras, was discovered. His description of the varied backgrounds of the miners of Independence bears repeating.

> The population of Independence represented almost every state in the Union, while France, England, Ireland, Germany and even Bohemia had their delegates. As soon as breakfast was dispatched all hands were engaged in digging and washing gold in the banks, or in the bed of the stream ... As for ceremony of dress, it gave us no trouble; we wore all alike. Shaving was voted a bore; the air holes in our pants were *not* "few and far between," and our toes as often as not out "prospecting" as any way, and from the ends of our boots a any way, and two weeks before my last supplies arrived, I was barefoot, having completely worn out my shoes.[443]

---

440 *Ibid.*, pp. 137–138.
441 *Ibid.*, p. 145.
442 *Ibid.*, pp. 146–150.
443 *Ibid.*, p. 153.

Later, Delano partnered with Timothy Ellsworth to buy a claim on Massachusetts Hill on Gold Hill in Nevada County. He organized the Sierra Quartz Mining Company. At last he began making profits from owning one-sixth of the Massachusetts Hill Quartz Mine. Under the company name Delano & Company, he worked hard to develop the mine and later sold out to Dr. J. C. Delavan, the agent for the New York firm Rocky Bar. He continued working as a storekeeper in several mining communities, including Grass Valley. He was elected the first treasurer of the City of Grass Valley.

* * *

First published in 1856, Delano's revealing, humorous collection of miners' anecdotes, *Old Block's Sketch Book, or Tales of California Life,* was illustrated by Delano's friend, the German artist Thomas Nast.[444] It was such a hit that, according recent historian Marquerite Eyer Wilbur, it inspired other journalists like Mark Twain and Bret Harte to produce classic California yarns that were popular throughout the world.

Beginning his foreword in the first person, Delano wrote,

> I had walked many a weary mile, had crossed many a deep gulch, had climbed many a difficult hill, when the shades of night began to close around me, and even hope had almost fled, when at last my eye caught the glimmer of light from a miner's cabin ... my knock and promptly answered, and the "Welcome stranger," sounded like glad tidings to my ears. "A stranger and they took me in—an hungered they gave me meat"—in trouble "they comforted me." My heart thanked them—my words seemed too barren.
>
> Dear reader—may I make an application of this 'o'er true tale?' Once upon a time thou hast opened the door of approval unto me, when the storm of doubt was whistling around. Twas then

---

[444] See the foreword by Marquerite Eyer Wilbur in the reprint *Old Block's Sketch Book* (Santa Ana, CA: The Fine Arts Press, 1947).

that thou took the stranger in and comforted him with thee again with more SKETCHES OF CALIFORNIA LIFE, hoping, but not daring, to ask for they approval. Thou surely dost not care, I am certain, whether I am engaged in the pumpkin and squash trash or not? Thou dost not care, I am certain, whether I bake my own flapjacks in my cabin, or board at Benton's Exchange, so long as I pay Benton my prog bill honorably every week? Thou dost not care if time and exposure hath marred my scalp-lock upon my crown and put spectacles on my nose, and no longer made me lovable to the ladies? And now will thou give thy hand to OLD BLOCK.

These words are as captivating today as they were when *Old Block's Sketch Book* appeared and came to be well read throughout the state and eventually the nation.

In his first chapter, he invites us as if we were newly arrived immigrants to the West, trudging along on a bitterly cold wintry day up a trail into a California mining camp.

The string is out at the door-you need not knock-just pull the string, the latch will raise, and the door open. Come in—sit down on that three-legged stool, and now look around and see how cozy and snug we are ... Before the fire is the bake kettle doing its duty, and the hot loaf is nearly done—you'll stay to supper and see what capital bread I can make. From a peg, near the fire place, hangs a frying pan, which we'll use presently to fry our bacon in, while on the floor stands the tea kettle, the coffee boiler and iron pot, that that is about all the cooking apparatus we want.[445]

---

[445] Ibid., p. 3. The character "Old Block" obviously is the fictional representative of Dalano himself. Delano's book is a similar genre to Mark Twain's and Bret Harte's works showing the funny side of California mining camp life. This book deserves to be resurrected and restored as the treasure of Americana that modern-day readers would love.

As California entered the mid-1850s, the gold rush began making profound effects upon the land and its population. Before gold's discovery in 1848, California was a remote province of Mexico. Its population was composed of a multiplicity of Indian tribes with about 150,000 members, about 6,500 persons of Hispanic or Spanish ancestry, around 80 non-native Americans, and a diffuse smattering of European-born and Hawaiian-born residents. By 1860, tens of thousands of new immigrants, most of whom could be roughly classified as forty-niners, were here. Females made up barely 15 percent of the total population. Indians were being killed off, or were dying, at such an alarming rate that many newspaper editors, reporters, and others feared they soon would be extinct.

Meanwhile, large mining companies bought out many individual miners' claims, changing the game into one only large companies with large capital reserves could afford to play. Hydraulic mining using huge pumps and high-powered hoses reduced hills and mountains into piles of rocks, shale, and ore.

Mines producing quartz, quicksilver, and mercury, each one a necessary element to processing gold bearing ore into pure gold bars, began operation. Mercury mines were beginning to pollute lakes and streams throughout the state, leaving a path of devastation that remains an unsolved dilemma for residents and their political leaders.

When he published *Old Block's Sketchbook,* Alonzo Delano, a storyteller, poet, merchant, and newsman, forcefully expressed his respect, affection, and love for his wife, Mary, and his fellow miners. He and other writers like Twain and Harte had no clue in 1856 what damage mining would do to the state's waterways and environment.

Considering relations of miners with the fairer sex, Delano wrote,

> When I was young I had the fortune—I don't know whether to write good or mis before it-to fall in love. No matter, I was in love. Well, every rhyme I made—and I made a good many of them strange enough too—I dedicated to the chosen one of my heart. It was she that gave me inspiration, and I couldn't for the life of me, write with anyone else in mind ... and I should feel as if I wanted to pick a quarrel with somebody, if I did not, so I now

with all my heart do, dedicate my little work TO MY FRIENDS,
THE MINERS OF CALIFORNIA THE AUTHOR.[446]

The miners were lonely, almost to a man. If they grew up in a happy, secure
home (like Nelson Kingsley), they yearned to be back wherever they grew up.
Everyone who swung a pickax or held a pan searching for gold yearned to settle
down with the girl of his dreams. In the cases of gay miners, they also wanted
a stable partner with whom they could share their lives. The desire was nearly
absolutely omnipresent. The simple problem was that one had to have a large
enough pile. Old Block was not shy about expressing his heart's desires.

Delano knew full well he spoke for many who realized the rough-and-
tumble life in the California mines would not be the place to bring a lady for
whom any mature, civilized man had feelings. Still, in his writing and for
effect, Delano allowed his emotions to flow.

But, after all, what would I give for a nice, pretty, sweet little
girl, just to—Pshaw! why should I wish to bring a fairy being,
to my cabin, to—make slapjacks and wash shirts, when I can do
it well enough myself. No, no: talk about love in a cottage, and
make as much poetry as you please, the fact is, bunk and hard
boards, fat bacon and beans, slapjacks and molasses, though
they have their sweets, are not exactly the place to put rosy
cheeks, ruby lips and laughing eyes in, for domestic comfort.
No, no; the cheeks would grow pale; the ruby lips would snap
with ire when the boys came in hungry to dinner, with sleeves
rolled up to the elbows, their old boots covered with mud, and
their dresses soiled and bespotted with the dirt of the drift.
Only think—when I should come out the claim after digging all
day, in a miner's plight, full of love and appetite, I should rush
up to my rosy cheeked darling, and, throwing my arms around
her fairy waist and placing my long beard and besmeared face
against her shy cheek exclaiming in the fullness of feeling—

---

[446] See dedication, *Old Block's Sketch Book* (Santa Ana, CA: The Fine Arts Press, 1947).

"Dearest, thy love was mine,

My only thought was thine—"

wouldn't I get a slap in the face from that lily hand, with a "Go along, you great, nasty brute? No, no" let the gal go till my pile enables me to get something more flashy than my cabin, and then—O get out![447]

The feelings expressed above by Old Block (Alonso Delano, a married man) might explain, at least in part, why even as late as 1860, it is estimated that only 15 percent of California's total population was composed of women. As has been well documented elsewhere, many of these were prostitutes or madams.

Near the start of *Old Block's Sketch Book,* Delano painted portraits of some of his cabin mates.

> Ned was a sort of universal genius. He could do anything, from singing Lucy Neal to baking a johnny cake—from writing a newspaper article to making a pump; and with a most generous heart, as careless of his money and jokes as a child. Always ready for fun, he was always ready to relieve distress, and never flagged in keeping up his end of labor; but he never went to town without spending half of his week's earnings-sometimes all-and when old Swamp good naturedly took him to task for his improvidence, he would explain, "I know I'm a fool, but how can I help it!"[448]

Ned was the kind of guy who was tough, strong, and proficient at many jobs, so he would have been a welcome member of any group of miners. His weakness was his tendency to spend his money unwisely, as Old Block mentioned. Delano also described an incident where a poor older miner appeared at their cabin door asking for a handout. Ned immediately wanted to lend him some from

---

[447] *Ibid.,* p. 4.
[448] Ibid., p. 5.

his own earnings. However, Ned's improvident ways had gotten him in trouble before. Before this, a wiser elder miner named "Old Swamp" had agreed to control Ned's funds for him. When the miner appealed to the miners for help, Ned's heart melted. He wanted to lend him money, but Old Swamp firmly stepped in and prevented him from doing so. This was the kind of anecdote that made *Old Block's Sketch Book* a literary hit throughout California.

Bogue Ejecting the Squatters.

Another character in Delano's work was Bogue, a hearty seaman turned miner.

> Bogue was a good fellow. He had seen thirty summers, but he didn't remember but twenty-six distinctly ... He had coasted through the first sixteen with the usual amount of flogging and

ferrule at school, and finally brought up at college, where he was regularly inducted into the mysteries of scrapes and punishments and in the course of two years' study took his degrees in robbing hen roosts and peach orchards, and could subtract a water melon from the patch, or a pin from the peddler's cart, equal to the most perfect masters of the art among his chums, and he obtained, by close application and unwearied diligence and deviltry, the leather medal awarded to the first in his class, and with it acquired the reputation of being the most daring rogue that ever slid down a rope from his window for a frolic.[449]

As his description of youthful pranks continued, eventually Bogue's hijinks caught up with him. After his expulsion from college without a diploma, Bogue had to take to the sea, at first as a common seaman. Despite reaching San Francisco as a first mate and having made voyages around the Horn, like many seamen, Bogue decided to give up his oceangoing life to become a forty-niner searching for gold.

One day we were busily at work in our claim; Bogue had got hold of a heavy rock, which he was intent upon getting out of the hole, when a neighbor made his appearance with the news that a company of three greenhorns had squatted on his claim, and were determined to prospect and work it for themselves, meeting his remonstrance with abuse and expressing their determination to work it "*viet armis*," if necessary. We knew that our friend, a quiet and peaceable man, was justly entitled to the claim by miners' law, and that such a proceeding on the part of loafers was unjustifiable by the statute miner, and Bogue, at once constituted himself judge, jury and posse committed, in the case, with an alacrity that might have done honor to Don Quixote himself.[450]

---

[449] Ibid., p. 9.

[450] Ibid., p.10. Delano's book showed the intergenerational everyday relationships, or at least some aspects of them. Bret Harte's stories were more revealing, including gay pairs of miners.

Bogue and the other miners (including Old Block) quickly moved to the claim that their friend had been at work on.

> On reaching the ground, sure enough, there were three gentlemen, in red shirts, with black pants, nicely strapped down under their books making most awkward demonstration with pick and shovel, apparently digging through as if they were on their way to visit their antipodes through a hole of their own making rather than Symmes'.

> "Avast there, ye lubbers," shouted Bogue, "you are cruising on ground under embargo without a permit. Up anchor and heave ahead, unless you want to catch a squall."

> "Who the d____l are you," replied one of the worthies, suspending operations, and looking hard at Bogue—"and what business is it to you!"[451]

This scenario of two groups of miners fighting over a claim was common throughout California's mining districts during the gold rush and after. Miners died defending by gunshot wounds in many cases. In this case, Bogue, as leader of the elder-in-status group, came back continuing using nautical lingo. Bogue's meaning came through loud and clear to the trespassers.

> "I'm Port Collector," returned Bogue, "and unless you can show clean papers, I'll throw my grapnells [grapnels] into your bows and rake you fore and aft in such a way as to not to leave a spar standing."

> "The mines are free, I reckon, Mister, and we have as good a right to work them as anybody," responded green-horn, in a

---

[451] Ibid., pp. 12–13.

half argumentative tone, "This ground is as much ours as it is yours."

"I've no time to spin yarns," echoed Bogue, "I'll give you just two minutes to come out of that hole, and if your hawser is not cut loose in that time, d_m[n] me if if there'll be a thing left on your deck from windlass to stern; I'll give your hatches and break bulk as I would for any pirate sailing under a flag as black as yours," and he deliberately took a chew from a pound plug and rolled up his sleeves.

"Boys," interlude Old Swamp. "You've heard the Captain's orders—mizzle. Or it will be worse for ye than a fire in a cane-brake."[452]

Led as they were by Bogue, the strong stand made to the greenhorns prevailed so that their friend retained possession of his claim. "So our neighbor was reinstated in his claim again, with an awful kind feeling towards Bogue."[453]

Each member of Old Block's group of miners gave to the others a unique strength or talent. As we just saw, Bogue was a strong man whose sense of justice and force of would came in handy to drive off the claim-jumping bullies. In addition to his positive attitude and work ethic, Ned played the fiddle, providing free entertainment. This helped them pass long, lonely evenings inside their cabin. Another important man was Old Swamp, a native of Kentucky who described himself as having been

rared in Indiana and come up on a plank." His father died when he was a boy, and the care of the family had early devolved upon him, and he discharged that important trust with a fidelity which was as rare as it was meritorious, and the necessity of

---

452 *Ibid.*, p. 13.
453 *Ibid.*, p. 13.

taking a common sense view of things was early impressed upon his mind.[454]

Under the heading "A Miner's Love Story," on a "dreary winter evening in December 1849,"[455] Old Swamp began telling his fellow miners the poignant tale of how he finally got married while still in Kentucky. As the Kentuckian told it, after he had set traps and failed badly in attempts to trap a gal for himself, he got his leg caught in a wolf trap on old Squire Beach's plantation one night.

> When the first I know'd, slap! went something with an almighty spring, and the teeth of a double power wolf trap dug into my leg, clean to the bone, 'Murder, murder—help, help—in the name of all creation!,' I shouted.[456]

Old Swamp's actual first name was Ambrose, or Am for short. The reason he was walking around the squire's house that night was in hopes of seeing the squire's daughter, Betsy.

> The Squire's dog set up a yell, and flew at me like a streak of lightning The Squire seized his rifle, and with the boys rushed out of the cabin. 'A wolf—a wolf—geet out Watch. I'll pepper the varmint.'
>
> "Take care, Squire; I'm dead-take care, it's me in the trap. It's me Squire; call off the dog, and don't shoot."
>
> "It's Am. Swamp," said one of the boys; "I know his voice—don't shoot father."
>
> "Am. Swamp!" said the old man, coming up. "what on airth are you doin' in my trap? Did you come to steal my sheep?"

---

[454] *Ibid.,* p. 14.

[455] *Ibid.,* p. 16.

[456] *Ibid.,* p. 22.

'No, not a single fleece,' said I, "open the trap, and let me out, and I will tell you all about it—oh! oh!"[457]

Old Swamp's wound was going to require nursing care and immediate first aid at the minimum.

> They opened the trap and let me out, but I couldn't stand. (So much for the trappin' gals, get trapped yourselves, sometime, boys.) I was much hurt.

> 'Take him to the cabin, boys,' said the old man. "Peter, run and tell Betsy to get some rags ready to bind up his legs. John, cross hands with me-there Am. Sit down, my boy. No matter how you got trapped we'll take care of you, Am."

> Now, old Squire was one of the kindest-hearted men in the settlement, and somehow he had always stood by me in trouble, and the boys, and was always ready to give me and mother advice and help, if we ever got bothered in the management of our affairs. I always thought a power of him, and I always liked Betsy, too, but I never thought of making up to *her*, for they were our nearest neighbors, and kind of in the family like.[458]

Am's (or Old Swamp's) road toward matrimony now took a different turn. His search no longer involved setting traps to get a gal. By then, as it does in every other romantic relationship where each person is serious in desiring the other,

> Wal, after they got me into the cabin, they laid me on the bed and examined my wound. It was an ugly thing, and the soft soap on my trousers made it smart orfully [awfully]. Oh, um! um! yes, it didn't do anything else.

---

[457] *Ibid.*, p. 22.

[458] *Ibid.*, pp. 22, 25.

> Betsy got some warm water and washed off the blood, and then
> wrapped a clean white cloth around the wound-but it ached all
> night. After I got a little easy, I just told the Squire the whole
> story from beginning to e'end [end], He couldn't help laugh'in
> [laughing], nor the boys neither; but I noticed that Betsy didn't
> laugh, but onst [once] I seed [saw] her wipe her eye with the
> corner of her apron-what for, thinks I?[459]

The squire's son John brought Am a suit of his clothes. Betsy took his clothes, washed them, and hung them out to dry. When they were dry, she laid them out by the fire.

> I didn't go home that night, and mother thought I was having
> first-rate luck, wondering all the while who it was that I had
> kotched [caught], and little dreaming, was kotched [caught]
> myself.[460]

So that was how Old Swamp, aka Am, found his wife, Betsy. Or was it the other way around? No real matter because marriage was all that really mattered.

What drove Old Swamp and the others to endure their hard life, "to battle with the climate and privation in every shape in our mountain wilds,"[461] was the dream "to give to those he loved better than his own life-comfort, happiness and independence."[462] What came of his life first in Indiana, then in upstate Illinois, before coming to California? According to Old Block,

Among other quirks of Old Swamp, he had a bright, blue-eyed, cheery-cheeked daughter, Jennie. She was about seventeen when Old Swamp left home for California with his stern resolution to relieve himself from embarrassment and place his family once more in independent circumstances—a proud and generous ambition that has warmed the hearthstone and household idols of home. Dear, dear Jennie was the idol of her father, and when he was praising her

---

[459] *Ibid., p. 25.*

[460] *Ibid., p. 25.*

[461] *Ibid., p. 25.*

[462] *Ibid.,p. 26.*

virtues, her intelligence, her industry, and her filial obedience, his countenance brightened up and the tear "sprung unbidden to the eye" as he added, "I'm an ungainly old brute, for her mother's child is as beautiful as an angel, and as good as she is beautiful."[463]

Although Old Block said "Jennie" was Old Swamp's chip, that wasn't her real name. As is still often the case today, Delano protected real persons by use of alternative names. After writing the above, Delano wrote that Old Swamp had received two letters, one from Jennie, enclosed in a cover letter from Betsy. His daughter wrote,

> DEAR FATHER—William Jackson has asked me to marry him. Father, I love him very much; but I told him I could not promise without your consent. Till I hear from you I shall remain, as I have been, and always will be,
>
> Your affectionate and dutiful
>
> JENNIE[464]

As Delano continued to present the discussion of how Old Swamp and his daughter would resolve this question, he explained that the old miner broke into tears as he thought of his love for his daughter. He replied to her that he would return to his former home as soon as possible, which probably would be May.

The matter was not settled quickly by Old Swamp, who actually left California, returning to his home by way of the Isthmus of Panama. Again, returning to the *Sketch Book*,

> It was about three months after our parting when I received a letter, directed "To Mr. Old Block, Esquire, Humbug Diggins, State of Calyforny, U.S.—_____ County,—with care and spede."

---

[463] *Ibid.*, p. 27. Delano's daughter Harriet, who later followed him to Grass Valley, may have been Delano's "Jennie," whom Old Swamp idolized.

[464] *Ibid.*, p. 23.

"Hurrah! For Old Swamp," I shouted, as I tore open the letter and read to this effect, for I have lost the letter and give it from memory:

> DEAR SIR AND FRIENDS, OLD BLOCK, ESQUIRE: I arriv at home ware I am at present, without accident only I found the steamer cussed poor stamping ground, ... Got down to Pennyma, whar the climat was so hot we lited our pipes by each others noses ... Wal, I weren't [wasn't] long in takin' a bee line for home, arter [after] I got to New York, whare [where] I am at present in my own cabin, with my wife Betsy on one side of me, and Jennie on t'other [the other], and my dog in the corner asleep.[465]

The letter continued with details of Old Swamp's interaction with Jennie's suitor, Bill Jackson.

> Jackson came over next day. Jennie turned as red as a cockses [cock's] comb, and made herself scarce the minnit [minute] he opened the door. 'Well Bill,' says I, "you want my gal, do you?" ... Can't coon in my cornfield, Bill. Jenny is goin' to Calyforny." I had a quirk in my head and wanted to try the varmint. "To Californy, Mr. Swamp! Oh, don't. Oh, Mr. Swamp, if you you on'ly know'd [knew]—I love your gal better nor all the men in the world," and he really looked like he did.[466]

The preceding exchange between the concerned dad and his daughter's prospective husband sent Jennie into a frantic state. Old Swamp asked for and

---

465 *Ibid.*, p. 29.
466 *Ibid.*, p. 30.

got in writing a parcel of Bill's "one hundred and sixty acres of land," for which Bill had been working to pay. In return, Old Swamp agreed not to return to California, taking his daughter along with him. Nevertheless, after sleeping on it one night, Old Swamp changed his mind. The letter ended in this way: "Bill and Jennie, my darling; dry your eyes and come here-there-there, Bill-take her—God bless you both. Yours till death, Ambrose Swamp." [467]

We never learn Old Swamp's age at this point, but his conscience made him see the light about how unreasonable it was to demand a land payment from Jennie's hardy, hardworking young suitor.

Following this heartwarming story of the elderly miner who always offered his hand to help a fellow miner like Ned, and other miners in need, Delano continued casually commenting.

SUNDAY IN THE MINES

Shall we hold the mirror to your gaze? Will you start at the reflection? I once went three months without taking a peep in the looking glass, at no time very inviting, absolutely made me stare at myself; a beard of three months growth, an old worn out hat, from which my matted locks were striking out in all directions, a greasy buckskin coat, wrinkled and dirty with unmentionables ditto; my toes peeping out into daylight from my old dilapidated shoes, like frogs from the scum of a pond. [468]

Delano's sketchbook description drew a stark contrast between a typical Sunday in the California mining regions with that of a Sunday in New England, the South, or the Midwest, where all businesses closed and the populace usually either passed its time at home, at some outdoor recreation (often at a picnic), in a park, or along a river or a lake. Many in the already established states also observed religious service under the auspices of a Protestant church, the Catholic Church, or at a Jewish temple on Saturday.

---

[467] *Ibid.*, p. 30.
[468] *Ibid.*, p. 34.

However, on Sundays, in this latest created state's mining regions (in the first half of the 1850s), it was not at all similar.

> That music is the squeaking of a fiddle; the tum, tum, tum of a banjo; the zee, zee, zee, thump of a tambourine, interlarded with the clickety-click of bones; or perhaps you hear the deep-sweet tones of a piano, discoursing some beautiful waltz of gallopade; that house is a gambling saloon, and the worshippers are those of Mammon, who would tempt the fickle Goddess of fortune by offering at her shrine the results of their week's labor, so hardly and so honestly obtained.[469]

Business and assay offices were generally open for business on Sundays, along with the gambling halls, bars and saloons, and brothels. For the miners who generally were hard at work six days a week, Sunday was the only day many could came to town to exchange gold dust or nuggets for currency. Towns located about ten miles from gold-bearing sites, such as Grass Valley, Yuba City, and Auburn, became commercial hubs.

By 1855, Grass Valley's population rose to 3,500 persons. Delano set down his roots in Grass Valley, where the townsfolk elected him the town's first treasurer. He had written articles as a correspondent for the *San Francisco Daily Courier* and the *Pacific News.* One of its foremost hotels located on Main Street was the United States Hotel, where it is believed the great fire began.

In picturing Grass Valley's devastating fire on the night of September 13, 1855, Delano wrote,

> Why, its being burnt down and built up again in a month, and coming out more fresh, more fair and beautiful than ever by the purification. As gold is more refined and bright by being submitted to the flames, so our towns are purified and rendered more beautiful than ever as they spring up from their own smoking ruins.[470]

---

[469] *Ibid.,* p. 37.
[470] *Ibid.,* p. 40.

Due in part to the fact that nobody had thought of the danger of fire to the growing mining town, Grass Valley lost over three hundred buildings, burned to the ground in one terrible night. In spite of residents' hard work in manning bucket brigades and wetting blankets, the town was almost totally lost. Delano, who was present at the time, the next day removed the town's bank vault and pulled it out from the smoldering embers.[471]

Eyewitness Old Block described the calamity.

> On the eventful night which laid our town in ruins, which left us no cover for our head but the blue vault of Heaven: when we were driven from our falling roofs to the streets, from the streets to hill, beyond reach of fire, there stood mothers with their children, and men ruined in purse by the catastrophe, gazing calmly upon the greedy flames, as they leaped from house to house, licking up their homes, destroying the result of years of toil, did you hear one word of wailing—one single note of despair? No, not one. Even females, who scarcely saved their garments coolly remarked, "It can't be helped; there's no use to cry, It's gone, and must be endured. We shall contrive to get along somehow."[472]

It was Alonzo Delano's mission to embrace his fellow miners, to help however he could, and to aid them in their many tasks. Like contemporary journalist authors Mark Twain and Bret Harte, among others, his published works left a mark that will stand the test of time. His books and his many published news articles told California's ongoing story as only an eyewitness could.

The rest of *Old Block's Sketch Book* is filled with more stories of miners and what occurred in the mining camps. Some have noted that although immense wealth was mined and brought forth into the world during the California Gold Rush, as the story of Old Swamp and his dear daughter Jennie shows, human nature doesn't change. People were the same here as they were anywhere else

---

[471] See Gary Noy, "The Grass Valley Fire of 1855," *Sierra College Press* 1, no. 1 (Winter 2008), accessed online March 23, 2017.

[472] *Ibid.*, p. 40.

in the world in the 1850s. The longer it lasted, the Gold Rush brought into the state more criminals, desperados, prostitutes, and others with low morals; they were a different kind from most of those first pioneers—individuals like Reverend Colton, Edward Prime, Edward Chever, and others who had arrived before it began or soon after it all started. This dangerous new element made it necessary for Californians to create vigilance committees, lawmen, and courts to restore law and order.

Unlike many forty-niners, Delano relocated in northern California, in the community of Grass Valley. He lived out the rest of his life there. However, Delano returned to New York to visit his family in 1851. When his first wife, Mary, died in 1871, Delano remarried a woman in California. His second wife's maiden name was Maria Harmon. She was a vivacious companion who was twenty years younger than he was.

He made another trip back east by way of Nicaragua to accompany his daughter, Harriet, who had become mentally ill in California.

Delano was a successful mine operator and co-owner. He worked for Wells Fargo as the Grass Valley's first agent. After his first wife, Mary, passed away in 1871, Delano remarried in 1872. Delano died in Grass Valley, where he had settled in 1874. He had referred to himself in his autobiography, cited herein, as a "nomad denizen of the world." He fulfilled the mission he had set for himself in 1848 when he'd left Illinois. When he passed, the entire town shut down and attended his funeral. He is buried at Greenwood Cemetery there.[473]

---

[473] See the biographical summary on Alonzo Delano, accessed online on December 20, 2015.

AFTERWORD AND ACKNOWLEDGMENTS

One of the reasons for writing this book is a question that first began perplexing me when I was a boy of eleven. It was 1953; the year before that, my father had moved our family to Lancaster, Ohio.[474] For him, this corporate transfer was a promotion. For my sister, Susie, and I, it was a great shock, wrenching us from the relative comfort zone of Lincoln Elementary School in Evanston, Illinois, to another elementary school in a strange town in a different state of the country.

The impetus for this book really began during my second year at North Elementary School in Lancaster, Ohio. I had been alphabetically placed in the front row of my fourth grade schoolroom, possibly because my last name began with the letters "Ba." The teacher was an experienced and dedicated pedant who drove her students through the founding of the nation, Ohio statehood, the nation's westward migration, "Manifest Destiny," and settling the Far West.

Sometime near the Christmas holiday, a question went unanswered in our general survey class, and the textbook was our only source of knowledge. Why did American citizens of all three regions of the existing States, at almost the same time (from 1840 to 1860), pack up their belongings, load them into carts and wagons, and leave their friends, jobs, and homes to embark on such a dangerous journey, mostly in covered wagons, bound for the Far West? This question remained at the back of my mind, hidden yet unanswered, while growing up and for many years afterward. Later in high school, the US history teacher emphasized, "We know very little about what really happened." Even

---

[474] My Dad. Frank H. Baumgardner, Jr., was a salesman who spent thirty-six years of his life working for the Anchor Hocking Glass Corporation, home office in Lancaster, Ohio.

after a graduate-level California history class at San Jose State University, this question persisted to elude me.

This book is my answer, going back primarily to the eyewitness accounts of the miners themselves (and why people came to California on the slight chance they would find gold). Oddly enough, there is a coincidental connection I have through Lancaster, Ohio, to Samuel McNeil, whose story is told in chapter 5. McNeil was born and raised where I also began my education, in Lancaster, Ohio, in southcentral Ohio. Today, it still continues to be a relatively small town in rural southwestern Ohio.

It was many years later, and half a continent west, that I made my initial trip to take my first job in teaching high school history at Bakersfield, California. My wife and beloved helpmate, Jeannette, attended UC Berkeley. Her roommate there was Alice MacBride. Nobody has helped me more than Mrs. Alice MacBride Schilla. Her editing allowed me to complete this original study. Her expertise in pointing out errors made by me when finishing each chapter was of inestimable assistance.

As ever, it was my wife, Jeannette Mahan Baumgardner (1943–2019). I'd be remiss if I did not also thank another of Jeannette's college friends, this time from her time at Dominican College in San Rafael, Gail Fraser West. My family—especially my brother-in-law, Larry Mahan; both my sons, Joel and Will; and my sister, Susie Baumgardner Kaiser—have stood by, listening in support. Patricia Keats, director of library and archives at the Society of California Pioneers Museum and Library, at the Presidio in San Francisco, led me to Edward Prime's diary, which I accessed during the summer of 2016.

Good friends Mark McDonnell, Bert Flack, and Glen Kennedy have helped in ways they may suspect but never fully realize. Thanks also to Saba Weldesclaassie, who was one of my wife's caregivers and who also accompanied me on a drive to Berkeley, California, to visit Bancroft Library for Nelson Kingsley's journal. Another friend, Steve Stedman, helped by lending me his great aunt Bertha S. Rothwell's Stedman family biographical summary, which is the source of Chapter 10. Robert Stedman was both a forty-niner and an expert woodsman and builder. Rosemary Bernard, Linda Sevier, and, last but by no means least, Kathleen Robards have all been a big help in the last crucial phase of getting this book together, including aiding me to find the cover image out of the thousands of images on Getty Images.

Lastly, the staff at Archway Publishing, starting especially with Michelle Wilhaite, Stephanie Frame, the editorial department, and Mrs. Sarah Smith, who aided me in publishing.

Frank H. Baumgardner III
Santa Rosa, California
December 8, 2019

BIBLIOGRAPHY

Adams, Charles F. *The Magnificent Rogues of San Francisco.* Palo Alto, Pacific Books, 1998.

Beilharz, Edwin and Carlos U. Lopez. *We Were 49ers: Chilean Accounts of the California Gold Rush.* Pasadena, CA: Ward Ritchie Press, 1976.

Buffum, Edwin Gould. *Six Months in the Gold Mines: From a Journal of Three Years Residence in Upper and Lower California, 1847-8-9.* Introduction by John W. Caughey. The Ward Ritchie Press, 1959.

Gudde, Erwin G., *Bigler's Chronicle of the West: The Conquest of California Discovery of Gold and Mormon Settlement as Reflected in Henry William Bigler's Diaries.* Berkeley: University of California Press, 1962.

Colton, Rev. Walter. *The California Diary.* Oakland: Biobooks, 1948.

Delano, Alonzo. *Across the Plains and among the Diggings.* Reprint of original edition with reproductions of numerous reproductions. Notes by Louis Palensky. Foreword and epilogue by Rufus Rockwell Wilson. New York: Wilson-Erickson, Inc., 1936.

Delano, Alonzo. *Old Block's Sketch Book, Drawings by Charles Nahl.* Foreword by Marguerite Eyer Wilbur. Layout and design by Thomas E. Williams. Santa Ana: Fine Arts Press, 1947.

Delavan, James. *Notes on California and the Placers: How to Get There, and What to Do Afterwards.* Foreword by Joseph A. Sullivan. Oakland: Biobooks, 1956.

Dolnick, Edward. *The Rush: America's Fevered Quest for Fortune, 1848–1853.* New York: Little Brown and Company, 2014.

Hale, Israel Foote. "Diary of Trip to California in 1849." *Quarterly of the Society of California Pioneers.* San Francisco: Society of California Pioneers Board of Directors, June 30, 1925.

Hale, Titus. "I Came with Him." *Quarterly of the Society of California Pioneers.* San Francisco: Society of California Pioneers Board of Directors, June 30, 1925.

Kemble, Edward. *Autobiography and Reminiscence of, Deceased 1901.* Written by an unnamed anonymous person, accessed online May 18, 2016.

Kidwell, Clara Sue. Homer Noley, and George E. Tinker. *A Native American Theology.* Maryknoll, NY: Orbis Books, 2003.

Kingsley, Nelson. *Diary of Nelson Kingsley, a California Argonaut of 1849.* Berkeley, CA: University of California, 1914.

Knochs, Elizabeth T. "A Study of Place Names in the American River." MA thesis, Sacramento State University, 1957.

Knower, Daniel. *Gold: The Story of the 1848 Gold Rush and How It Shaped a Nation.* New York: Thunder's North Press, 2005.

INDEX